SPECI

Why It Is Wrong and the

Implications of Rejecting It

Copyright © 2015 Magnus Vinding

First paperback edition 2017

All rights reserved.

ISBN: 154651032X
ISBN-13: 978-1546510321

CONTENTS

	Introduction	1
	Part I: Why Speciesism Is Wrong	
1	Why Speciesism Is Wrong	5
	Part II: The Implications of Rejecting Speciesism	
2	Embracing Veganism	23
3	Abolishing the Property Status of Non-Human Animals	27
4	Vivisection	30
5	Granting Proper Moral Consideration to Non-Human Animals in Nature	40
6	The Conservationist Delusion	46
7	Intervening in Nature — An Imperative	50
8	Intervene How?	65
9	A Short Note on Insects	74
10	Transcending Speciesist Language	82
11	Is Anti-Speciesism Anti-Human?	87

Epilogue: We Are All Speciesists	89
What You Can Do Now	94
Acknowledgments	95
Bibliography	96

INTRODUCTION

We are ethically deluded. There are thousands of billions of sentient beings on Earth who all experience, feel, enjoy, and suffer, yet our firmly established consensus is that only seven billion of these *really* matter — those who belong to the human species. *"We must do what is best for humanity!"* our collective moral tune goes, and in almost all we say and do, we chant and promulgate this anthem of moral confusion. This cannot be defended. We must include all sentient beings in our sphere of moral concern, regardless of which species they belong to. We must go beyond speciesism.

What is speciesism?

Speciesism is discrimination against beings based on the species they belong to. To be more precise, speciesism is, as philosopher Oscar Horta writes, *the unjustified disadvantageous consideration or treatment of those who are not classified as belonging to a certain species.*[1] Hence, to reject speciesism is to reject the notion that beings matter less because they belong to a certain species, and to instead

---

[1] For elaboration on this definition, see Horta's article *What Is Speciesism?*
Link:
https://masalladelaespecie.files.wordpress.com/2010/05/whatisspeciesism.pdf

prioritize the well-being of sentient beings on the basis of their sentience alone.

There is a lot of confusion about the concept of speciesism, and the perhaps most common confused idea about it is that a rejection of speciesism implies that we must treat alls beings the same, for example that we should give all animals, human as well as non-human, the right to vote. But this is silly. Prioritizing equal interests equally does not imply that we should treat beings in the exact same way, for the simple reason that different beings have different interests and needs. Therefore, different treatment does not necessarily amount to discrimination, i.e. *unjustified disadvantageous treatment*. Just as it is not sexist to treat men and women differently in certain regards — for instance, to only offer women screenings for cervical cancer, or to only offer men screenings for prostate cancer — it is not speciesist not to grant non-human animals the right to vote, since they, like human toddlers, cannot meaningfully do so.

In fact, if anything follows from the rejection of discrimination, including speciesism, it is exactly that we *should* treat different beings differently, since such a rejection indeed requires that our treatment of different beings be based upon their different individual abilities, interests, and needs. Only on a speciesist or otherwise discriminatory view could we ignore these.

The aim of this book is to examine our speciesism. This examination consists of two separate parts, where the first part shows why speciesism is unjustifiable, and hence why it must be rejected, while the second part examines the practical implications of this rejection. This latter examination is bound to be far from exhaustive, and bound to leave many important questions untouched, since there are both too many questions, and too many uncertainties related to these questions, for them to all fall within the scope of this short book. As we shall see, however, merely pointing out the most basic and most important implications of the rejection of speciesism reveals more than a few ways in which our behavior and attitudes, our worldview even, should change, and change profoundly.

PART I

WHY SPECIESISM IS WRONG

WHY SPECIESISM IS WRONG

One of the defining traits of the moral progress of humanity in the last few centuries is that we gradually have distanced ourselves from discrimination in its many forms. Where it was once the norm that the rich Caucasian man above a certain age had rights that nobody else had, while women and people of certain ethnicities had no rights at all, we have finally come to realize that such discrimination is deeply unethical. We have finally realized that racism, sexism, ableism, and other forms of discrimination against human beings cannot be justified. Not that they do not exist anymore — they do indeed — but they are no longer as widespread as they were 200, 100, or even 50 years ago, and they are now widely regarded as indefensible. We have finally realized that women should not be given fewer rights because they are women, that people should not be discriminated against because of the color of their skin, and that people who have a disability should not be treated with less care and respect because they have a disability. When it comes to humans, we have finally realized that it is by virtue of sentience alone — the fact that we are conscious beings who can experience suffering and well-being — that we are inherently valuable in moral terms. When it comes to humans, we recognize that this and nothing else is the true basis of moral concern. Black, white, male, female, physically or cognitively impaired or not, it is all irrelevant for our status as beings of inherent moral value, beings who should be respected and treated as ends rather than means.

Having realized this much, the question that is now staring in the face of humanity is this: why have we confined this insight to humans only? Why, when it comes to non-human beings, is it suddenly as if we are back in time, failing to realize that sentience alone is what makes a being morally valuable? Why are we still defending diminished concern for non-human beings — even defending that we mutilate and kill them for frivolous reasons, such as palate pleasure — with reference to the very traits that we recognize to be morally irrelevant when it comes to humans? Indeed, why does speciesism still stand as strong and unchallenged as ever?

Whatever the reason may be, it is not a valid one. Speciesism is wrong, and it is so for the same simple reason that other forms of discrimination, such as racism, sexism, and heterosexism, are wrong: because it amounts to a diminished moral concern for beings based on a morally irrelevant criterion. Just as an individual's race, sex, or sexual orientation is ethically irrelevant, it is not morally relevant which species a sentient being belongs to. As we realize when it comes to humans, we should always recognize that individuals have inherent moral value, and prioritize their lives and well-being *on the basis of their sentience alone* — not their race, gender, sexuality, intelligence *or species*. (And for this reason, what I refer to as "non-human animals" throughout this book is actually *sentient* non-human animals. Which beings are included in this category is an open question, but, as I have argued in *A Copernican Revolution in Ethics*, it only seems reasonable to maintain that all vertebrates and at least many invertebrates, such as cephalopods, are sentient. Beyond that, the question becomes harder, yet we should generally aim to err on the side of caution.) To do anything else is to engage in discrimination against certain beings — to give them *unjustified disadvantageous consideration*.

The wrongness of speciesism is really that simple, and actually requires no further elaboration. Nonetheless, the conclusion that speciesism is wrong clearly has a hard time gaining acceptance, and countless desperate attempts have been made to reject it so as to preserve the gap between human and non-human beings that presently exists in our moral perception. The remainder of this chapter is a refutation of the most common of these attempts.

"Discrimination against non-human animals is not ethically unjustifiable. Human beings and non-human animals are different. Humans have cognitive capacities that other animals don't have. Humans are far more intelligent."

Human beings are surely different from non-human beings, but men are also different from women, and people who do not have certain mental abilities are also different from people who do. The point being that mere difference obviously does not justify disadvantageous consideration. The contrast between our view and treatment of humans who do not have certain mental abilities and our view and treatment of non-human animals who also do not have certain mental abilities is especially striking and worth contemplating in this context. For we obviously do not find it defensible to grant less moral consideration to a human if s/he does not have certain cognitive abilities that most other humans have. On the contrary, we rightly realize that we often have an even greater obligation to help them than we have to help most other humans, as they often need help and assistance more. When it comes to humans, we rightly realize that individuals should be granted full moral consideration regardless of their notional "intelligence level", yet for some reason we fail to realize that exactly the same applies to non-human individuals.

This reveals a clear double standard in our thinking, and it shows that this anthropocentric objection against speciesism is not a sincere one. Because if we really held that beings who do not possess certain cognitive capacities should not be granted full moral consideration, then we would also maintain this view with regard to humans, yet we all recognize this to be unacceptable.

It is not that intelligence and other abilities, such as the ability to help others, are not morally important — they are indeed — yet this is where the distinction between intrinsic and extrinsic moral value becomes paramount. The well- and ill-being of sentience is the basis of intrinsic moral value, and for this reason, whatever factors and abilities that can affect sentience positively, such as altruism and intelligence, also have positive moral value, yet their value is *extrinsic*: they are not valuable in themselves, but to the extent they contribute to the well-being of sentient beings. And in this regard humans may be claimed to have the potential to have greater extrinsic value than other animals in general, as humans may have a greater potential to help other beings than other animals do. Yet it is worth noting that we also have the greatest potential extrinsic *dis*value; that is, we are also the kinds of beings who are capable of causing the most suffering in the world.

However, differences in the extrinsic value that beings may have can also be found between human individuals, and the important thing to point out is that a being's greater *ex*trinsic value does not grant such a being greater *in*trinsic value. Again, intrinsic value only comes down to sentience, and is thus entirely independent of a being's extrinsic moral value.

"Non-human animals do not belong to the moral community since only moral agents belong to the moral community, and non-human animals are not moral agents. The fact that children and some adult humans lack moral agency is irrelevant, because children will grow up to be moral agents eventually, and adults who do not display moral agency are simply broken moral agents."

This objection fails on every level. A natural question to ask in light of this objection is that if a human individual's lack of moral agency can be dismissed as irrelevant via the belittling move of calling them "broken", why can the same not be done when it comes to non-human animals? What is the relevant difference? Yet to pose this question is already to grant too much to this objection, because it is simply not the case that only moral agents belong to the moral community. As the objection itself acknowledges, beings who are not moral agents also belong to the moral community, which calling such individuals a denigrating term like "broken moral agents" does not change. As we all recognize when it comes to humans, moral agency is not a requirement in order to be worthy of moral consideration — only sentience is (cf. the discussion of intrinsic and extrinsic moral value above). Objections like the one above overlook this, and hence express a very troubling view of our fellow humans, and indeed

9

completely miss what it is we value in our fellow humans, including children and adults who may not be moral agents. For, as philosopher David Pearce has noted, "we value young children and cognitively challenged adults for who they are, not simply for who they may - or may not - one day become."[2] And, one may add, not because of the abilities they would have had were they not, in the words of T. R. Machan, "deficient" or "broken".[3] As a case in point, we all realize that a baby with a terminal illness whom we know is not going to live beyond her second year still belongs to the moral community and deserves moral consideration nonetheless, which should make it obvious that this claim that humans belong to the moral community because they are either potential or "broken" moral agents is wrong and morally misguided.

Lastly, aside from being irrelevant, the claim that non-human animals are not moral agents is also plain false. For instance, in one experiment,[4] monkeys were willing to starve themselves for the sake of saving their fellow monkeys from getting electric shocks — a display of morality and care that surely tops the moral sense of those who devised this experiment to discover something that observational studies in nature surely could have revealed. After all, in nature, monkeys do more than merely make sacrifices to avoid harm to their fellow group members: they collaborate, groom each other, and

---

[2] Pearce, 2013. Link:
http://www.hedweb.com/transhumanism/antispeciesist.html

[3] Machan is one of the few people who have openly defended the exclusion of non-human animals from the moral community: "invalids are, as it were, deficient or borken [sic] moral agents [...]" Quoted from:
http://www.amazon.com/review/R1WCLG3573SUV1/

[4] Masserman et al., 1964.

exhibit many forms of self-sacrifice and altruism.[5] And this is of course not unique to monkeys, as many social mammals display what most of us would identify as moral behavior.[6] Yet again, this gross factual error is beside the point, as it is still only sentience, not moral agency, that is the requirement for moral consideration, as we all recognize when it comes to humans.

"It does not matter what abilities a human or a non-human may or may not have. What matters is the kind that a being belongs to — beings who belong to humanity are those whom we owe full moral consideration."

Whether humans deserve special moral consideration — and, more generally, whether "kind" is ethically relevant — is the very thing in question here, and to state that this is the case more or less by definition is merely to opt out of the argument and to choose the poor road of question begging.

Second, it should be noted that this same objection could also be used to justify other forms of discrimination, such as racism and sexism, if one defines "kind" to mean race or gender. A racist could say that what matters is whether individuals belong to a certain race, and that only those who belong to a certain race deserve full moral consideration. Fortunately, most of us reject this claim as the expression of bigotry and primitivism it surely is, yet the argument is no less primitive or bigoted when used to argue against granting non-human beings full moral consideration. As we recognize when it

---

[5] Examples of such behavior has been documented in the works of authors such as Frans de Waal, Marc Bekoff, and Jonathan Balcombe.

[6] See for instance Churchland, 2011.

comes to racism, it does not matter where one is positioned on the family tree of living beings, only sentience matters, which leads us to the third reason why this objection is absurd: it is wrong about the basis of the value of human life, and it is therefore also degrading toward humans.

For the truth is that human individuals are not valuable because they are human, and it would indeed amount to a denigration of the value of human life to say that they are. Rather, human individuals are of intrinsic moral value because they are *sentient*. After all, would we humans lose our inherent moral value if we suddenly no longer happened to be humans by any common definition (and as we shall see below, this is not an impossible scenario), or would we lose our inherent value if we lost our entire experience, including the potential to ever have any experience — essentially, if we died? It should be clear that the answer is the latter.

It is also worth noting that the meaning of the term 'species' is itself unclear; it is a folk notion that does not have a single, clear meaning. This would be especially clear to us if our extinct relatives of the genus *Homo* had still been alive today. Did these relatives belong to another species than our own? By some definitions, some of them did not, since humans could have fertile offspring with them, for instance Neanderthals. By other definitions, they were another species. The question then becomes: would discrimination against such beings of another branch of hominids be speciesism or racism? This is where we see that the line between the two is bound to be unclear and ill-defined, and that speciesism is not qualitatively different from racism: they both amount to discrimination against our sentient relatives, the only difference being how distantly related these relatives are. It shows that anyone who opposes racism without also opposing speciesism has taken up an arbitrarily narrow fight against discrimination, a fight that will inevitably be grossly discriminatory itself.

Lastly, the supposed separateness of different species becomes even more problematic in light of modern biotechnology. With the advent of genetic engineering, it is now possible to insert genes from one species into individuals of another species, and hence to create beings with multi-species DNA (the same thing has happened naturally, albeit in more random ways, throughout the history of life, which further underscores the blurriness of the concept of discrete species). In principle, a hybrid between, say, a dog and a human is possible, and this poses deep problems for the anthropocentric speciesist. For would such a hypothetical being deserve full moral consideration? Or only half?

To spice this thought experiment up with a bizarre twist, imagine that we have a human baby whom a mad scientist decides to gradually morph into a dog-like being by virtue of continual insertion of genes from a dog. Will this baby, on the anthropocentric speciesist view, eventually no longer deserve full moral consideration? And if so, at what point? An anthropocentric speciesist may respond that it does not matter what a human baby becomes, and that no matter how much any scientist molests a human baby, the morally relevant "seed of human dignity" will always exist in this being who was at least once a proper human. In response to this, we can simply revert the thought experiment: imagine that we have a being who was born as a dog, or who was perhaps a dog zygote, and then, through genetic engineering, a mad scientist gave this dog distinctly human features, including human language and moral reasoning. Which moral status would such a being have on the anthropocentric view? Full moral consideration eventually? At which point? This breakdown of what it means to belong to a species in light of the possibilities of modern technology only serves to underscore the inevitable breakdown of speciesism upon closer examination, and to expose its indefensibility.

"In life-or-death situations such as the burning building scenario, most people would choose to save a human rather than a non-human animal, and this is not wrong. Therefore, speciesism is not wrong."

This is merely a distracting non sequitur, since differences in priority in such cases of serious conflict do not justify discrimination in general. After all, most people would likely also choose to save certain humans over others in such a situation — for instance, to save children over old individuals — yet such prioritizing does not remotely justify reduced moral status of anyone. In the case of saving younger people over older people, the fact that we may choose in this way does not in the least justify disregard for old people. The exact same holds true in relation to non-human beings. No matter which beings we may choose to save first in a burning building scenario, we should still give full moral consideration to all individuals, and still help relieve their suffering and promote their well-being as much as we can.

Invoking the burning building scenario to defend speciesism is simply yet another rationalization employed to defend the status quo, one that we would never use to argue for reduced moral concern for any group of humans.

"But speciesism is not indefensible. There are relevant differences between humans and non-human animals, namely differences in the degree to which they are sentient. Humans have a large brain with a large cerebral cortex, and therefore a greater capacity to experience suffering and well-being. This justifies greater moral concern for humans than for non-human animals."

The claim that humans are more sentient, meaning that humans experience a greater range of suffering and well-being, than other animals is disputable to say the least. On what basis can we assert that a mouse or a fish feels pain any less intensely than humans do? The fact that they have smaller brains provides no such basis. After all, children have smaller brains than adults, but should children feel pain or joy any less intensely than adults? It appears they do not, and the opposite could well be the case. The truth is that we have no reason to believe that a larger brain, be it in terms of its number of neurons or in terms of its mass, necessarily gives rise to more intense experiences. Sure, it seems reasonable to expect that there is *some* relationship between brain complexity and the quality and intensity of the experiences a brain can give rise to, yet this does not imply that bigger brains necessarily give rise to more intense experiences than smaller brains, just as we cannot say that beings with bigger thighs necessarily run faster than beings with smaller thighs, even though there surely is some relationship between thigh-size and running ability. Humans for instance have larger thighs than domestic cats, but that clearly does not imply that we can outrun them. Similarly, it might well be the case that our larger brain does not have more intense experiences of pleasure and suffering than does the brain of, say, domestic cats, or any other animal with the relevant brain structures. Indeed, as Steven Pinker notes, "we have every reason to believe that cats suffer as much as humans do."[7]

Our investigations of the relationship between brains and conscious experiences indeed give us little reason to believe that the number of neurons found in the brain is of the greatest relevance when it comes to the intensity of experiences. For instance, we know that more than half of the neurons in the human brain are found in the cerebellum, a brain structure that does not seem to play a big role for our conscious experience, if any at all, while a minority is found in the cerebrum whose activity most aspects of our conscious experience, if not all, seem to depend upon. Hence, what seems most relevant with regard to the capacity to experience is not the number of neurons found in the brain, but rather certain brain structures — the basal ganglia and other structures found in the cerebrum — and these structures are found across the vertebrate line, and analogous structures are found in many invertebrates.[8] They are anything but

---

[7] Quoted from: https://www.youtube.com/watch?v=ooTcyioNIZ4.
Pinker mentions cats as an example; his point pertains to all beings with the relevant brain structures.

[8] See for instance the so-called Cambridge Declaration on Consciousness, which notes that simple states of consciousness may have arisen long before vertebrate species arose, which implies that conscious states may be shared not only by all vertebrates, but also by many invertebrates too. It also states that:

> The absence of a neocortex does not appear to preclude an organism from experiencing affective states. Convergent evidence indicates that non-human animals have the neuroanatomical, neurochemical, and neurophysiological substrates of conscious states along with the capacity to exhibit intentional behaviors. Consequently, the weight of evidence indicates that humans are not unique in possessing the neurological substrates that generate consciousness. Non-human animals, including all mammals and birds, and many other beings, including octopuses, also possess these neurological substrates.

uniquely human.[9]

And not only may other beings feel such experiences as intensely as humans do, they may even experience sensations such as pain more intensely. As evolutionary biologist Richard Dawkins has noted, a reasonable argument can be made for the latter proposition:

> [...] I can see a Darwinian reason why there might even be a negative correlation between intellect and susceptibility to pain. [...]
>
> Isn't it plausible that a clever species such as our own might need less pain, precisely because we are capable of intelligently working out what is good for us, and what damaging events we should avoid? Isn't it plausible that an unintelligent species might need a massive wallop of pain, to drive home a lesson that we can learn with less powerful inducement?

---

[9] It is not that we humans are not unique neurologically and cognitively — we are indeed — but our uniqueness does not seem to lie in our capacity to feel joy and suffering. We are unique in that we, for example, can communicate verbally, contemplate and execute long-term decisions, and perform mathematical calculations. However, these abilities do not seem to enhance the vividness and intensity of experiences in general, much less be requirements for them, which they surely are not. There is, after all, a great deal of variation in the above-mentioned abilities among us humans, and some humans are even completely without these abilities. Should such human beings feel feelings any less intensely than the mathematical genius who can communicate ideas effectively and plan rationally? We have no reason to believe they do. Ditto for the non-human animals who have the relevant neurological structures that underlie pleasure and suffering. We must admit that these beings likely are our equals, many of them perhaps even our superiors, in the ability to experience suffering and well-being.

> At very least, I conclude that we have no general reason to think that non-human animals feel pain less acutely than we do, and we should in any case give them the benefit of the doubt.[10]

So we should at least acknowledge the possibility that non-human animals may be feeling sensations such as pain even more intensely, and suffer even more from them, than humans do. But even if we assume that the smaller brains of most non-human animals make them less sentient than humans, this would still not justify not taking them and their well-being seriously in moral terms. After all, there are also humans who have much smaller brains than most humans. For instance, some humans are born without cerebral hemispheres,[11] which means that, according to the reasoning behind the objection above, it is justified to grant such humans less moral concern than we grant other humans. Again, that such persons should be less sentient than other humans is highly disputable, and the opposite cannot easily be ruled out: that humans without cerebral hemispheres may experience many sensations even more intensely than other humans. Second, a majority of us will likely disagree with this claim about granting such individuals less moral consideration, regardless of whether they are less sentient in any sense. However, let us here for the sake of argument push it and say that we adopt this view that humans who do not have certain brain structures do not deserve the same moral consideration as other humans do. What

---

[10] Dawkins, 2011.

[11] For instance, some children with hydranencephaly have no cerebral cortex at all: http://www.ncbi.nlm.nih.gov/pubmed/18435419

would the implications of this view be? The answer: next to none. Because whatever granting "less moral consideration" means in this context, it is clear that all humans are of intrinsic moral value, beings whom we should do what we can to spare from avoidable suffering; that we should protect, prioritize, and take seriously their lives and well-being; and that their fundamental interests should never be trumped by the trivial interests of others.

So the acceptance of the controversial claim that humans who do not have certain neurological structures do not deserve the same moral consideration as humans who do have these structures — a claim that few are willing to defend in the first place — does not in any way dispute that we should take such beings seriously in moral terms and grant their interests concern, and, needless to say, this applies to all sentient beings who do not have certain neurological structures, not only humans. To deny this is to engage in discrimination based on species membership and nothing else, which is exactly what the objection above attempts to distance itself from.

The thing that objections that invoke differences between humans and other animals, including differences in sentience, to defend reduced moral concern for non-human animals seem to consistently miss is that whatever difference one may claim to exist across different sentient species just as reasonably can be claimed to exist across different human individuals. Yet when it comes to humans, few are tempted to make these same arguments so commonly made in favor of less moral consideration for non-human animals. For instance, the claim that some humans are less sentient than others is a very rare one, even though this intra-species claim is at least as defensible as the equivalent inter-species claim, and far rarer still is it to hear any argument that holds that supposedly less sentient humans deserve less moral concern. It is difficult to ascribe this asymmetry to anything but speciesism.

The root source of our speciesism is not so much our disregard for purportedly less sentient minds, however, but more that we embrace a kind of "bodyism" — an ethic of human bodies in particular. Because, after all, we would never find it justifiable to morally disregard and kill a being with a human body just because s/he has the mind of a cow or a chicken, or any other kind of mind, so why do we find it okay to morally disregard and kill a cow or a chicken because they have the mind of a cow or a chicken? It cannot be the mind that is the determining factor. Clearly, our moral intuitions are animated by a "human bodyism" of sorts, and it is thus clear that if we transplanted the brain and mind of any non-human animal into a human body, this would — cf. the observation above — protect this being from our speciesism. And this perfectly exposes our ethical failure on this point, since it of course betrays one of the most fundamental ethical values we all hold, namely that *we should not value a being differently based on the body/the external appearances that being has.*

Yet that is exactly what we do. When it comes to non-human animals, we still see the outer appearance as relevant. We fail to connect with the conscious subject, and we justify our discrimination more or less in the same way as we justified our racism and sexism in the past: because they are black, they don't have the same rights, the white folks said, and because they are women, they don't have the same rights, the men claimed. Today we put non-human animals into the x of this equation of discrimination: because they are non-human animals —

because they have fur, tails, or feathers — they do not deserve full moral consideration, we say, and we are just as wrong in this case.

Speciesism is indeed unjustifiable and indefensible. Again, speciesism is *the unjustified disadvantageous consideration or treatment of those who are not classified as belonging to a certain species*, which means that to the extent that non-human animals are less sentient than humans, or vice versa, such a difference may be morally relevant, at least under some circumstances. But again, the following must be pointed out: first of all that we have no basis for asserting that humans are more sentient — that we suffer more and experience sensations more intensely — than our sentient non-human cousins, and, second, that whatever such differences there may be, these do not remotely justify any moral disregard toward sentient individuals of any kind, just as any variation in sentience there may be in humans does not justify disregard for any human individual. As we realize when it comes to humans, we should prioritize and protect the life and well-being of all individuals. We should grant proper moral consideration to everyone, whatever family, race, *or species* they belong to. That is why speciesism is wrong, and that is why we must reject it.

PART II

THE IMPLICATIONS OF REJECTING SPECIESISM

EMBRACING VEGANISM

The most obvious implication of the rejection of speciesism is that we abolish the exploitation of non-human animals and embrace veganism. What this means in practical terms is, among other things, that we do not eat or wear non-human animals. The only reasons we have for wearing and eating non-human animals are frivolous ones[12] — that we like it, that we are lazy, that it is a habit etc. — and, as we all realize when it comes to humans, these reasons do not remotely justify that we raise, confine, or kill other individuals. We do not accept the exploitation and killing of other humans for such frivolous reasons, no matter what cognitive abilities they may or may not have, and our failure to see that such exploitation is no more justifiable in the case of non-human animals is merely an expression of speciesism.

Indeed, anything short of a strict commitment to veganism amounts to both an expression and a reinforcement of speciesism. To see that this is the case, it is worth turning our attention to what our attitude is with regard to eating or wearing humans. For instance, we would never be tempted to wear the skin of certain groups of people, or to claim that it is extreme to avoid wearing such skin, citing that the

---

[12] See the first chapter of *Why We Should Go Vegan*.

person whose skin it was is dead anyway, and therefore that wearing their skin causes no harm. For the truth is that it indeed would cause tremendous harm if we suddenly began to find it acceptable to wear the skin of certain groups of humans. It would morally denigrate these humans in a way that not only fails to reflect the value of the lives of these people, but which powerfully undermines it. A glance at history proves this much: those who have killed humans and made items out of their skin surely did bring extreme harm upon humans, and unavoidably so, given the view of people that such behavior reflects and reinforces. Wearing the skin of a killed human is simply not compatible with a minimum of respect or moral consideration for that human, or for humans in general.

The exact same is true when it comes to wearing non-human animals: when we wear the skin of beings such as cows or goats, we inevitably undermine any moral clearsight with regard to these beings, we reinforce a view of them as beings whom it is perfectly fine to exploit and kill, and we thereby inevitably cause harm to them. We need to end rather than reinforce this tendency, which at the very least requires that we become strictly committed to not wearing or otherwise consuming anything made from their bodies. Anything short of that will continue to reinforce a morally defunct view of non-human individuals rather than challenge it.

And this applies not only to wearing and eating non-human beings, but also to the consumption of things derived from them while they are alive, such as dairy and eggs. For just consider how outraged we would be if we treated humans like we treat cows in our dairy industry. It seems safe to say that we would never accept a practice that forcefully makes women pregnant every year and which takes away their babies right after birth — the boys being killed soon thereafter and the girls being bound to have the same fate as their mothers — in order for us to get milk from these women, no matter how much we enjoy drinking milk or are unable to "give up cheese". Nobody would consider supporting this industry a matter of personal choice.

Yet this is exactly the horror story that is unfolding in the dairy industry that most of us happily throw our money after. This is what we do to cows whom we have every reason to believe experience as bad pain and suffering from their pregnancy and labour, not to mention the violent insemination they are subjected to, as a human would, which clearly reveals that we have a double-standard whose source is pure speciesism. If only the cows in our dairy industry had human bodies, people would no doubt be outraged about such an exploitative practice of human-looking beings, and they would no doubt demand the highest punishment for those responsible. Unfortunately, the reality is that they have cow bodies, and that we are all responsible for the continued thriving of this industrialized torture.

The dairy industry is of course just one example, and the specifics about our exploitation of non-human animals are actually irrelevant in relation to the main conclusion. Because, again, we all recognize that it is wrong to enslave, raise, kill, or in any other way exploit humans for trivial purposes such as palate pleasure or fashion preferences, no matter what kind of mind they may have, and nothing but speciesism prevents us from realizing that the same is true when it comes to non-human individuals. Simply stated, anything but a strict commitment to veganism — anything but the refusal to support, and participate in, exploitation of non-human individuals — amounts to speciesism. There is nothing that reinforces our speciesism more powerfully than our daily habitual use and consumption of non-human animals and things derived from their bodies. It is the cardinal sin we commit, as it comprises an insidious form of propaganda against non-human individuals, a propaganda that makes us inclined to deny that they even have minds and are feeling individuals,[13] which in effect causes us to ignore the atrocity we commit against them, and to defend it even. For we are naturally inclined to try to defend and rationalize our habits, which means that as long as we make the products of the suffering and death of non-human animals a daily part of our lives, we will inevitably be inclined to rationalize and defend the death and suffering of non-human animals rather than oppose it.[14] We will inevitably fail to feel that there is anything wrong with speciesism, which is why veganism is the first step we must take in order to go beyond speciesism.[15]

---

[13] Bastian et al, 2012.

[14] As a case in point, consider the example of the dairy industry mentioned above, or the egg industry that, among other horrible practices, grinds male chicks alive. Such atrocities would surely have gone viral were it not for the fact that it is our own habits that cause them to happen, which means that opposing such atrocities without changing our own habits would make us hypocrites. And since we don't want to change our habits, and since we don't want to be hypocrites, all we hear is silence and embarrassing rationalizations.

[15] And it is worth noting that not eating or wearing animals or things from them is not sufficient. We must strive to make our food production casualty-free, which our current production of plant foods is not, as we for instance kill rodents during harvest. These harms should not be trivialized merely because they happen in the context of food production.

ABOLISHING THE PROPERTY STATUS OF NON-HUMAN ANIMALS

Our time will no doubt be seen as a strange one. A time where people could all agree on the wrongness of human slavery, and on how unbelievable the moral delusion of previous generations had been in this regard, and still these people of the early 21st century saw absolutely nothing wrong with non-human animals being property; nothing wrong with the owning, using, and killing of sentient beings, as long as they did not belong to the human species.

It is indeed strange why we consider the ethical question of human slavery one of the easiest ones we ever had to answer — the answer was, and is, *no, it cannot be justified* — while we also consider the question of non-human slavery one of the easiest ones to answer, and the strangeness of course lies in the fact that we provide the complete opposite answer to this second question. Why this remarkable difference? In short, speciesism — because they are not human.

Thus another obvious implication of the rejection of speciesism is that we should abolish the property status of non-human animals. Once again, the analogy to beings with human bodies should make this clear: we would never deem it acceptable if beings with human bodies could be owned, bought, and sold as commodities, no matter what kind of mind they may have, and no matter how well we treat them in the process. We all recognize that such practices cannot be justified. However, the body is still not an ethically relevant characteristic, and there is therefore no valid reason to not consider the property status of sentient beings with non-human bodies profoundly wrong too.

The reason it is wrong to have sentient beings as property, more specifically, is that it gives these beings a status as things rather than a status as the sentient individuals they are, and, consequently, if we keep sentient beings as property, we will inevitably treat them more like things than like beings. We will treat them as means rather than ends. And that is exactly what we do: we own and sell non-human beings, and in the quest for profit that buying and selling them is, their well-being will generally only be a concern to the extent it serves this financial goal. Sentient beings and their well-being, or lack thereof, inevitably become mere means for economic gain in practice. That is inevitably what happens when we turn beings into commodities: their value is reduced to being instrumental rather than intrinsic, and this is a mistake guaranteed to cause harm. This is why we reject the property status of humans, and why we should also reject the property status of non-human beings.

"Does this imply that we should no longer have "pets"?"

There are many problems related to our practice of "pet" ownership. For instance, millions of healthy non-human animals are killed in shelters every year because of this practice, and millions more are neglected by their owners and treated in horrible ways — some are tortured to death. But would recognizing the moral status of non-human beings necessarily require us to not have them in our homes? Again, thinking about how we feel about humans, beings regarding whom our moral thinking is more finely tuned, can help shed some light on the issue. When it comes to humans, we do not accept the practice of breeding for the purpose of making good children for adoption, as this practice also amounts to a commodification and objectification of humans, and to making humans means rather than ends. Neither should we accept this practice when it comes to non-human beings, as it amounts to the same thing: it is a practice that overlooks the individual and his or her well-being, and which turns non-human animals into means rather than ends.

This is not to say that we should never bring non-human animals into our homes, however. For just as adopting a human child who needs care is a good thing, so is adopting a non-human being who needs care, of course given that one can provide the adopted being a good life. And it seems obvious that we should not bring more beings who are completely dependent on us into existence as long as there are already countless non-human individuals whom we have brought into existence and who need our care to live a decent life. There are millions such beings living in shelters right now, and we indeed have an obligation to adopt and help them, and to not treat them as mere property.

VIVISECTION

Richard Ryder, coiner of the term 'speciesism', was perhaps the first one to point out the significant inconsistency that underlies our practice of vivisection: we experiment on non-human animals with the justification that they resemble us very closely, and then we morally justify these experiments with the statement that they don't resemble us very closely.[16] A devastating observation.

The truth is that there indeed is an asymmetry, but that it goes the other way: we know that the bodies of non-human animals are in many ways not representative models for the human body and its mechanism (see for instance Knight, 2011, part II), whereas we have no solid basis for asserting that the morally relevant characteristics of non-human animals — e.g. their ability to feel pleasure and pain — are different from those of humans in any relevant way. Indeed, as mentioned in the first part, we have every reason to believe that other animals can suffer as much as humans.

This should render the unsurprising core foundation of our current practice of vivisection clear: speciesism. If any doubt remains on this point, one need only point to the simple fact that we do not accept

---

[16] Ryder, 1972.

non-consensual experiments performed on humans, no matter what traits they may have. Whether they have cerebral hemispheres or not, whether they have a family that cares for them or not, whether they live to see their second birthday or not, we agree that human individuals should not be subjected to non-consensual experiments, even though human bodies resemble human bodies more than the bodies of non-human animals do. So how can we defend this double standard of accepting absolutely no non-consensual experiments on humans, while we do accept such experiments on non-human individuals? We can't.

An observation worth making in relation to the subject of vivisection is how confused most people are about its moral status. For while large parts of the population are against vivisection, it is only a tiny minority that is strictly committed to veganism, and from an ethical standpoint, this makes no sense. Vivisection is a practice that, at least in some instances, is not merely done for obviously frivolous purposes, while practices such as eating, wearing, and otherwise using things derived from non-human animals are all done for merely frivolous reasons. There is absolutely no necessity involved in these latter practices. So how does it make sense to oppose vivisection, which is at least sometimes done for the purpose of saving, i.e. extending, human or non-human lives, while financially supporting the exploitation and killing of non-human animals for frivolous reasons such as taste, habit, or convenience? It doesn't. One simply cannot be opposed to unnecessary harm to non-human animals and then not embrace veganism, not consistently anyway.

And when one looks at the numbers, the disproportional focus on vivisection compared to the attention we pay to the exploitation of non-human animals for frivolous reasons only becomes more bizarre, since the former only accounts for a tiny fraction of the suffering we impose on non-human animals, while our use of non-human animals for frivolous purposes, such as eating and wearing them, accounts for the vast majority. Not that vivisection does not cause enormous amounts of suffering — we subject more than 100 million non-human vertebrates to experiments every year. But this all pales in comparison to the number of non-human animals who have to suffer and die because we "like the taste", as we kill more than 50 billion land-living non-human beings, and far more aquatic beings, *every year* in order for them to be eaten, and these beings often live lives that are just as bad as, and often far worse than, the beings who are subjected to vivisection.

This is the deeper problem with our exploitation of non-human beings: we are so used to exploiting and killing them that we do not see it as a fundamental problem that we do it in the first place, and we therefore do it casually. We have become morally numb to the suffering and death of, at least many kinds of, non-human beings. This is also the underlying problem with our practice of vivisection: we claim that we should only do it when necessary, yet how can any estimate of necessity be trusted when we find it acceptable to exploit and kill non-human beings for overtly frivolous reasons?

Thus, the problem of vivisection only serves to further underscore the importance of veganism, because as long as we exploit non-human beings and put them in our mouths and on our bodies for frivolous reasons, we will obviously not think clearly about vivisection, and any objection against it will be inconsistent and hypocritical.

But where does this leave us with regard to vivisection today? What if one is willing to bite the bullet and claim that experiments on non-consensual humans are justifiable? After all, could one not argue that it is justifiable to sacrifice one human for the sake of saving ten? And if it is, should we not in fact start experimenting on non-consensual humans? The answer to this question is "no" — for various reasons. First of all, it is never the case that any experiment is guaranteed to save anybody. There is usually great uncertainty as to whether an experiment carried out on somebody will even be useful in any way, which means that to carry out an experiment on someone, human or non-human, is often little more than a shot in the dark. And most of us would agree that we cannot justify sacrificing humans as such shots in the dark that may or may not be useful, no matter what traits and abilities these humans possess or don't possess. In other words, virtually no one is willing to actually bite the bullet and come forth and defend and advocate for the use of humans in biomedical experiments, which reveals that our moral intuitions on this matter are very much animated by speciesism.

Once again, the thought experiment of body substitution might help expose this speciesist intuition. For we would hardly ever consider it okay if beings with the mind of a mouse and the body of a human were used in a painful medical experiment that might hold some promise to promote human medicine, and yet we allow it routinely when the mouse mind inhabits a mouse body, even though the body is still not an ethically relevant criterion, and even though a mouse body obviously is a far less reliable model for the human body than an actual human body is. Human "bodyism" is clearly playing with our intuitions here. But is our resistance against subjecting humans and beings with human bodies to vivisection really all that reasonable? Yes.

There are indeed good reasons to oppose vivisection on humans, not only because it harms the individual human who is experimented upon, but also because it harms our moral attitude with regard to humans in general. A crucial piece of the jewel that is our respect for human life would be destroyed if we accepted non-consensual experiments on humans. And the exact same is true when it comes to non-human animals: when we subject non-human animals to vivisection, we not only harm the individuals whom we vivisect, we also undermine fundamental moral respect for other members of the species that this individual belongs to, and thereby reinforce speciesism. In other words, accepting such a practice prevents any deep respect for the kinds of beings whom we vivisect from developing in the first place, and there can be little doubt that the huge difference between our attitudes toward vivisection on humans and our attitudes toward vivisection on non-human individuals comes down to the respective presence and absence of such fundamental respect.

Consider by analogy if we began to find it acceptable to perform vivisection on people of a certain race. Is it not obvious that having a protective fence of fundamental moral respect — i.e. rights — in place with regard to people of one race that prevents non-consensual experiments on these people, while not having such a fence in place for people of another race is going to lead to terrible outcomes for the group of beings whom we have not established such fundamental moral respect for? And is it not especially problematic when beings of the privileged group are performing vivisection on the unprivileged group, while justifying these experiments with the claim that they serve the greater good? It should be clear that the privileged group in this thought experiment acts immorally, and that its claims about sacrifices for the greater good should be met with intense skepticism. Substitute "another race" for "another species", and this is no longer a thought experiment, but our world as it is.

So what to do in a world full of disease and suffering, most of which can only be cured by scientific and technological progress?[17] The question is a difficult one, but upon rejecting speciesism, it becomes clear that we should take the same approach to non-human animals[18] as we take to humans: we should do what we can to cure their ills, but not by subjecting them to vivisection, which they should have the right

---

[17] It should be noted that there are many things we already do know that could improve health dramatically. For instance, improved diet, increased exercise, and increased condom use could no doubt save millions of human lives annually.

[18] Including insects? Like the problem of vivisection itself, this question deserves an entire treatise of its own, and I shall not provide a satisfying treatment of it here, but, to put it briefly, I would regretfully argue "no" for various reasons. Consider consistency, for instance: one would have to ban walking on grass before it would make any sense to ban vivisection on insects, and vivisection on insects surely holds much greater promise for the reduction of insect suffering than grass walking does, which is not to say that vivisection on insects or walking on grass — an act that potentially causes much more suffering than, say, boiling a lobster alive — are morally unproblematic; they surely are not.

But is this not speciesist against insects? It can be argued that it is not. Insects often only live ten days or less, and we generally do not disallow experiments on other species, including humans, at similar stages of complexity. So in this way, on a view that looks at complexity and nothing else, it is arguably not speciesist per se to allow vivisection on insects such as fruit flies, which is still not to say that vivisection on insects and embryos are not morally problematic — they unquestionably are, and the only thing that can justify it, if anything, is that it will reduce suffering.

not to be subjected to.[19] As we do in the case of humans, we should instead employ alternatives to vivisection, and thanks to science and modern technology itself, there are now many such alternatives, and new ones continue to emerge. Simulations, for instance, comprise an especially promising set of tools, and they exist in many different forms, from human-like dolls to computer simulations. These tools can assist in everything from health care training[20] to the development of new drug therapies among other things,[21] and, in the case of computer simulations, they have the distinct advantage that the data is easily obtainable — it is right there in the computer, ready for analysis.

Another promising method is in vitro testing on human cells and tissues, which, in relation to applications for human health, have the distinct advantage that they are actually human cells and tissues. This is yet another example where modern technology compels us to abandon barbaric and unreliable practices, since human tissues and cells are both better models for human tissues and cells than the cells and tissues of other animals are, and since human skin in itself obviously does not feel any pain, which makes testing for things such

---

[19] Tom Regan arrives at a similar conclusion — that we should abolish vivisection — from a rights and anti-speciesist perspective in the following piece: http://tomregan.info/criminalizing-vivisection/.
Regan's argument pertains to mammals, whereas I maintain we should grant the right not to be subjected to vivisection to all beings whom we can be reasonably sure are sentient, including all vertebrates and more complex invertebrates such as cephalopods.

[20] See for instance: https://www.youtube.com/watch?v=ZchlovEQ4YU
This is obviously in a very early stage, and these simulations will surely become more refined over the next few decades.

[21] See Greek & Greek, 2004, and Knight, 2011, part III. See also: https://www.youtube.com/watch?v=Mg2fJ0UBj_0&t=24 for a good example of what happens when innovation and invention meets medicine.

as skin irritation entirely pain-free. And while already quite advanced, these techniques are still far from fulfilling their promising potential, especially in terms of adoption, which is bound to change over the coming years, if for nothing else, then at least for economic reasons, as these methods become cheaper every year.[22]

Lastly, it should be noted that abolishing vivisection does not mean that we can no longer conduct any research that involves non-human animals. In fact, it is vitally important that we conduct such research and study non-human animals, because in order to take their interests into consideration in our actions — which a rejection of speciesism requires us to do — we obviously must have sufficient knowledge about what their interests and needs are in the first place.

One important method for obtaining such information is observational studies, observations of non-human animals who live in the wild or in our care, and, as hinted earlier, such studies can no doubt provide many of the same insights that are sought in behavioral studies where non-human animals are confined in a lab, while also providing many insights that a lab setting can not. Furthermore, one can also gain valuable information from procedures performed on non-human animals for the sake of their own well-being, by monitoring blood tests, biopsies, and reactions to treatments conducted for the sake of their own health, just as we do in the case of humans.

---

[22] For instance, the costs of genome sequencing, which, while not the same, is still closely related to *in vitro* methods and what we can do with them, have plummeted in a way that no other growth in technology, including the growth of the power of computers, comes even close to matching: http://www.genome.gov/images/content/cost_megabase_.jpg

In conclusion, the abolition of vivisection on non-human animals[23] will not mean the end of medical and scientific progress, just as abolishing vivisection on humans did not have that consequence, or anything close to it. Yes, abolishing experimentation on both non-consensual human and non-human beings no doubt implies that certain procedures that could otherwise be carried out can no longer be performed, even if they could produce useful results, but that does not force science to a halt. Rather, it forces us to develop alternative methods that are more ethical, and these methods could well end up providing even faster and more reliable results that end up saving more lives and reducing more suffering, both for non-human and human individuals.[24] This is what we do if we reject speciesism. This

---

[23] As noted, what I refer to by "non-human animals" in this book is *sentient* non-human animals, and in this particular context, it is those non-human animals whom we can be reasonable sure are sentient: vertebrates and complex invertebrates such as cephalopods (cf. the note on insects above).
So am I claiming that other invertebrates such as insects are insentient? No, but this is where thinking in terms of a continuum of sentience and complexity becomes paramount. Evolution fosters continua, not strict lines, and with thousands rather than millions of neurons, insects arguably resemble human embryos in terms of complexity and sentience. And we do perform experiments on such embryos, not out of bigotry, but because they are in a stage of development where we deem the complexity and the likelihood of the presence of sentience small enough to justify experiments on them. One can dispute whether this indeed is justified, but given that we do it on humans, it can hardly be deemed speciesist. And with regard to whether it is justified, it should be noted that the reasons we do these things are not frivolous ones, which separates the avoidable stepping on/eating of oysters, insects, and embryos (or, more realistically in this latter case, not wearing a condom) from experimenting on them.
Any position one takes on the question concerning where to draw the line is bound to be controversial and worthy of harsh criticism, including the one I have taken above, yet in my own view, it seems the least bad one.

[24] And it is indeed important that we spend our resources in the best way

is the future we should pursue.[25]

---

possible, and not merely in ways that most would consider "better than nothing". For instance, to save thousands of human lives by subjecting hundreds of non-human individuals to vivisection is often proposed as being acceptable, but if we with the same means could have saved millions by sacrificing none instead, this would no doubt be better on any view, and it would clearly render the former action not only "not good" but beyond unacceptable and immoral by all reasonable standards. When non-human animals are the victims, we tend to overlook this perspective. When the victims are human, we never miss it — *there has got to be better ways, and if not, we will invent them!*

[25] Andrew Knight reaches the same conclusion from a somewhat different, and much more elaborate route in his book *The Costs and Benefits of Animal Experiments*, in which he, based on a utilitarian analysis of the available data that weighs the benefits of vivisection against the costs, concludes that the benefits are not worth the costs.

GRANTING PROPER MORAL CONSIDERATION TO NON-HUMAN ANIMALS IN NATURE

If we reject speciesism, it should not need pointing out that we must take the suffering of non-human beings seriously no matter where it occurs. It does not matter whether non-human individuals find themselves in a human society or in nature — their suffering matters regardless. Unfortunately, it seems that this point actually does need pointing out, and perhaps even more so than any other, since even people who otherwise show great concern for non-human animals, and who strive to transcend speciesism, often fail completely to realize this: that we should also take the well-being of non-human animals in nature seriously.

Traditionally, most theories of rights for non-human animals have only called for the abolition of humanity's use of non-human animals, i.e. called for the negative right of non-human animals to not be exploited by humans. And while this is no doubt an important and necessary step, it is far from sufficient. In fact, to only advocate for this right and nothing more is speciesist, since we would never take the same approach to humans. In the case of humans, we realize that we not only have negative duties toward others, we also have positive ones. We not only have obligations to not harm others ourselves, we also have obligations to prevent them from being harmed in other ways. For instance, if a human is about to be eaten by a lion, we realize that we have an obligation to help that human, and that a failure to do so amounts to a total moral failure.[26] To not realize that the same is true when non-human animals are the victims, including lions themselves,[27] simply amounts to speciesism. In other words, the idea

---

[26] For anyone who doubts this, the following video-link is provided to put that doubt to shame. The video shows a man who gets eaten alive by lions (WARNING: Disturbing images):
http://www.abolitionist.com/reprogramming/maneaters.html
Thousands of humans die in a similar fashion ever year — by being eaten by predators — as do an untold number of billions of non-human individuals. In this case, interference was not possible, but is there any doubt that not interfering in such a situation when intervention is possible would amount to a total moral failure? The same applies to the non-human animals who are killed in this manner every second.

[27] Lions also kill and eat each other (WARNING: Disturbing images):
https://www.youtube.com/watch?v=UBfMfqx5pUs;
https://www.youtube.com/watch?v=NB81Q3_Xs64;
https://www.youtube.com/watch?v=18muVT1GWqM;
https://www.youtube.com/watch?v=aA8YiZrYBg0.
The point being that interfering with lions' and other predators' killing and eating sentient beings alive is not a matter of anti-lion or anti-predator bigotry in any way, since lions and other predators themselves are also victims of such acts. And it should be noted that these are not unique incidents. All the lions in the footage above are most likely dead by now, and have likely either been eaten alive themselves or starved to death and then eaten. Nature is generally nasty for sentient life.
I would very much have preferred not to refer to footage of such horrible character, but the dogma of "happy nature" is unfortunately often so strong, and our abstract idea about what it means to be eaten by a predator so weak, that it takes something stronger than mere words to change our minds on this subject. The point is that nature is full of suffering, and that it is indefensible to insist on leaving it alone. If one accepts this much, there is no point in torturing oneself with horrible images of this kind.

that we do not have an obligation to help prevent harm for non-human animals, including those who live in the wild, is a deeply speciesist one.

The theorists and advocates who defend the rights of non-human animals while maintaining that we should generally leave non-human animals in nature alone suffer from more than just speciesism, however.[28] Another form of discrimination is also going on. For when it comes to the non-human animals whom we currently exploit, these people all agree that we have obligations toward these beings that go beyond abolishing our exploitation of them, and beyond not harming them. We also have the obligation to prevent them from being harmed and to provide good lives for them. For instance, in the case of zebras who live in zoos, everyone seems to agree that we should not "liberate" these beings by letting them go free on a field full of lions. We all realize that we cannot defend letting these beings in our captivity suffer such a horrible fate of being hunted and eaten alive. Yet, strangely, if these beings do not live in human captivity, but instead already find themselves on such a field, these same advocates will insist that not only do we not have an obligation to prevent them from suffering such harm, we have an obligation not to interfere at all. And notice that one cannot defend this double standard by saying that the non-human individuals in our captivity cannot "make it" in the

---

[28] It seems that most advocates for the rights of non-human beings and thinkers concerned with the broader subject of "non-human ethics" hold views of this sort, and follow Tom Regan's claim that "our ruling obligation with regard to wild animals is to *let them be*." (Regan, 2004, p xxxvii), including Peter Singer, "we should leave them alone as much as we possibly can" (although he seems to have changed his mind on this subject recently: https://www.youtube.com/watch?v=rrhBJlxKqyA), and Gary Francione, "we should simply leave them alone" (both quoted from Donaldson and Kymlicka, 2011, p. 159). Notable exceptions include Oscar Horta and David Pearce.

wild, because the zebras who get eaten in nature are clearly just as unable to "make it" as those who have grown up in captivity would be. No, there is no valid defense for this double standard, which springs from a view that gives greater concern to beings who live "in our care"[29] than to beings who live in the wild — inadvertently, no doubt. Merely because she grew up in nature, we have no obligation to save the frightened and wounded zebra who is about to be eaten alive by a lion, while had she only grown up in our care, we would have such an obligation according to the most mainstream views among advocates for the rights of non-human individuals. There can be no doubt that this view is a discriminatory one, a view that grants *unjustified disadvantageous consideration* to a certain group of beings. Yet it is clearly not species per se that this form of discrimination comes down to, since we are not talking about different species of non-human animals here.[30] Rather, this form of discrimination is better described as *ferism*[31] — discrimination against beings who live in the wild merely because they live in the wild (*fera* is Latin for 'wild animal'). And needless to say, this is no better than discriminating against beings based on their position in society (arguably, in the

---

[29] One can argue where the line goes for which beings who count as being domesticated/living in our care and who do not, and it is worth noting that the line is much less clear than many seem to believe. For example, on which side of the line do pigeons and ducks who are fed daily by humans find themselves? What about non-human animals in zoos? Are they domesticated or wild? Both "neither" and "both" seem defensible answers.

[30] Still, the attitude that we should leave non-human individuals in nature alone is a speciesist one, as we would never hold it in the case of humans. Again, most of us realize that we should save a human who is about to be eaten by a lion.

[31] In an earlier version of this book, I called it *feraism*, but Oscar Horta pointed out that *ferism* is a better word: it "sounds better and is easier to pronounce."

broadest sense of 'society', it is identical to this). It is just as unjustifiable as discriminating against beings based on their gender, race, or species.[32]

Contrary to what our immediate moral intuitions may hold, beings are no less worthy of moral concern and protection merely because they live in nature. To care more about seven billion people than about the tens of billions of non-human animals whom we exploit is clearly speciesist, yet to care more about ten billion non-human individuals who are victims of human exploitation than we do about ten billion non-human individuals who live in nature is also morally deluded.[33]

---

[32] A good example of ferism (and speciesism) among activists who are purportedly against speciesism is their release of minks into nature. While such actions may seem noble at first sight, especially given the gruesome fate that awaits these minks, it is hardly that noble from the perspective of the non-human animals whom the released minks will go out and eat in nature. These activists would hardly release minks into a cage full of live mice, yet that is in fact exactly what they do, modulo the fact that the cage full of mice and other vulnerable non-human individuals that they release the minks into is nature. This perfectly exposes the ferism of such actions — the ignoring of certain non-human victims *because they live in nature*. Also, these activists would hardly release predators in a zoo in order for them to go out and kill and eat humans, including small children, which exposes the speciesism of these release actions — a disregard toward the non-human individuals that the minks will kill in nature that these activists would never show toward humans. The wish to help minks who suffer the horrible fate of being victims of human oppression and violence is of course more than noble, but what we must do is spread anti-speciesism, because from that, veganism, including the end of such horrible practices, follows directly (for elaboration on this point, see Oscar Horta's talk 'On Strategies': https://www.youtube.com/watch?v=v_vsHlKZPFQ). The alternative short-term solution of releasing them only leads to harm for other beings in nature and causes more minks to be brought into existence and suffer a horrible fate, meaning that this short-term "solution" is not at all that.

[33] This is not to say that it does not make sense to focus disproportionally on the non-human individuals who are victims of human exploitation in practice, both because their suffering is created and perpetuated by us, which means that ending it should be relatively easy, and also because we are unlikely to

Couple this with the fact that there are more than a thousand times more non-human animals in nature than in human captivity, and it becomes clear how misguided — and how anthropocentric, actually — it is to only focus on the non-human animals who are victims of human exploitation.

The bottom-line is that we must include non-human animals who live in nature in our sphere of moral concern too, meaning that we must also take their suffering seriously. Indeed, until we do this, our moral view with regard to non-human animals will not only be lacking, it will be a complete failure, since, again, about 99.9 percent of them live in nature.[34] Until we take the non-human animals who live and suffer in nature seriously in moral terms, we can hardly claim that we take non-human animals and their suffering seriously at all.

---

[34] take non-human individuals in nature seriously in moral terms until we stop exploiting, wearing, and eating non-human beings. But in terms of intrinsic moral importance, beings weigh no less on the moral scale simply because they live in nature. I shall return to this issue in a subsequent chapter.

See: http://reducing-suffering.org/how-many-wild-animals-are-there/.

And this is just counting vertebrates. If one counts small invertebrates such as insects as well, the fraction of non-human animals who live as human property becomes far smaller still.

Our ignoring the suffering of non-human animals in nature is hardly difficult to make sense of. First, because we have grown up watching it every day (for instance in the form of starving birds) without even recognizing it as being bad, or even recognizing it as being suffering in the first place. Second, our ignoring the suffering of trillions of animals in nature also makes perfect sense in light of the work of Paul Slovic (see for instance Slovic, 2007), who has documented that when numbers get big, our moral sense gets small, nay, entirely dysfunctional. Indeed, any number of individuals beyond one is hard for us to think clearly about in moral terms. So if there is a moral problem we were born to ignore, it is surely the suffering of non-human animals in nature. But unfortunately, as we shall see in the next chapter, we have managed to turn this bias into a normative principle that takes the form of a "nature is good and should be left alone"-dogma. This is a delusion we must transcend. For more on this moral blindspot, see Ben Davidow's essay 'Why Most People Don't Care About Wild-Animal Suffering'.

THE CONSERVATIONIST DELUSION

Before we proceed further with the problem of suffering in nature, it is worth first turning our attention to the prevailing ethical stance when it comes to nature, namely the ethic of species conservation. For in order to advance our ethical stance with regard to non-human individuals in nature, we must first dismantle and clean out the confused and misguided ideas that currently dominate our views on this front. And there is surely no idea more dominating and more confused in this sphere than the idea that the most important moral mission we have with regard to nature is to try to conserve the species that presently inhabit Earth.

The ethic of species conservation is indeed a bizarre one. It is a view that holds the conservation of populations of certain kinds of beings to be more important than the well-being of the individuals in these populations. It essentially amounts to the reduction of non-human individuals to being mere means to the end of keeping some kind of status quo in nature. There are two obvious problems with this view, the first being that there is no such thing as a status quo in nature in the first place. The "natural state" of nature that we are asked to conserve was never a "conservational" one in the first place, and least of all at the level of species, since 99.9 percent of all species that have ever lived on Earth are now extinct.[35] Different species of life have arisen and disappeared constantly. *This* has been the natural state of things for the entire history of life, which implies that, ironically, our effort to conserve nature — which usually means nature as it is *right now*, or perhaps a few decades or centuries ago — is in some sense a most unnatural one.[36]

The second and even bigger problem with the ethic of species conservation is that it is starkly unethical and speciesist, which should be obvious if we again shift our focus to humans. For in the case of humans, we would never be tempted to spend resources to try to conserve certain kinds of people — e.g. a certain race of humans — as doing so clearly would amount to a failure to see other humans as ends in themselves, and a failure to understand the core aim of ethics. For what matters is sentient individuals and their well-being, not the preservation of certain kinds of individuals. This is all plain common ethical sense when it comes to humans, of course, yet when it comes to non-human beings, we have turned a profoundly speciesist ethic into unquestioned, and almost universally praised, (im)moral dogma, an ethic that overlooks individuals, and which takes the worst kind of instrumental view of non-human animals.

Thus, the rejection of speciesism clearly requires that we abandon

---

[35] Raup, 1992, p. 10.

[36] The view of an unchanging nature that underlies the conservation ethic betrays the religious roots of this now unquestioned ethic.
One may object that humans are presently causing extinctions of species at an unnatural rate, yet this objection begs the following questions: 1) what does "natural" mean in this context? And, 2) what makes any supposed "natural" rate of extinction normative? (And it should be noted that mass extinctions have been seen before, yet that is actually beside the point, as the question stands regardless: what makes the "natural" normative?)

47

the ethic of species conservation and realize that it is no more defensible to strive to conserve species of non-human kind than it is to conserve human races — that conservation of kinds of individuals, whether human or non-human, simply is not the aim of any sane ethical stance. And it is indeed bizarre that we seem to show deep concern for the existence of some beings, for instance orangutans and panda bears, just because they belong to a threatened species, while we at the same time directly support the exploitation and suffering of other beings, such as chickens and fish, just because they belong to another species.[37] Our speciesism could hardly be clearer. A speciesism that the ethic of species conservation not only fails to question, but which it actively reinforces and perpetuates.

"But is species conservation necessarily speciesist? Are certain species not required for the health of ecosystems?"

Yes, having species conservation as a goal in itself is necessarily speciesist. It is not a defensible ethical goal if we take beings of other species seriously in moral terms, only their lives and well-being is, and everything else is and should be instrumental to *that*, never species

---

[37] It is of course rarely true concern we show for non-human animals like orangutans and panda bears either, as we rarely care about individual orangutans or pandas. When it comes to non-human animals, we have for some reason made 'kind' into the object of moral concern, especially in nature, where it seems that, as Oscar Horta has noted: "[…] nonhuman animals are usually considered not as individuals but as mere live exemplifications of a species (because of widespread speciesist attitudes)." (Horta, 2010, p. 9.) And to tie our ethical confusion back to vivisection, it is clear that if a given group of non-human animals were very threatened, we would not perform vivisection on them. Panda bears are not in danger of being subjected to vivisection, and the same would likely be true of rats and mice if only they were rare. That, not their unthinkable suffering, appears to be the only thing that could save them from the extreme horrors we impose upon them, which perfectly reveals our ethical confusion on this matter.

conservation per se. Again, is aiming for the conservation of certain human races for the sake of conservation necessarily racist and unethical? Does such an effort to conserve races for the sake of not losing "biodiversity" reflect a proper ethical view of other beings? Hopefully these questions answer themselves.

As for the health of ecosystems, this question merely echoes the speciesism of species conservation. Can we defend preserving or reintroducing groups of humans because they contribute to some conception we may have of biodiversity or a healthy ecosystem?[38] Clearly not, as such a view again amounts to an instrumentalizing view of humans rather than a view that regards humans as ends in themselves. And the exact same applies to non-human animals: we cannot defend prioritizing what they may add in terms of "biodiversity" higher than we prioritize them and their well-being. To do so is nothing but speciesism in action, albeit in the guise of an ethical attitude that is widely praised and embraced. We need to start caring about sentient beings and their well-being first and foremost, no matter what species they belong to, and no matter how much we would like them to contribute to biodiversity.[39]

---

[38] And it is worth noting that a "healthy ecosystem" is very much a folk notion. Nature strictly has no health and has no preferences. The same is not true of sentient beings.

[39] The clash of ideas between the conservation of nature and the protection of the well-being of sentient beings is no doubt one of the most important ones of all, as the winner of this clash not only will determine the future of sentient life on Earth, it might determine the future of life in the entire universe, or at least in our future light cone, and either cause it to be free of suffering or fail to.

INTERVENING IN NATURE — AN IMPERATIVE

"Pain is a powerful motivational tool, and evolution has no qualms about using it to maximum effect."

— Brian Tomasik

The conservationist delusion and the notion that our overriding obligation with regard to nature is to leave it alone[40] seem to both arise from the misconception that nature, if only left untouched by humans, is a happy and idyllic place. Unfortunately, this idyllic view of nature is false, and, largely for that reason, it is also speciesist, because only from a speciesist perspective can one fail that hard to make the slightest attempt to examine what life is actually like for the vast majority, i.e. more than 99.9 percent, of non-human animals on the planet.

Life in nature is indeed full of suffering. Horrors such as being eaten alive — either from outside by predators, or from the inside by parasites — starving to death, and suffering and dying from disease

---

[40] It is worth noting that these two beliefs are in fact hardly compatible, which renders their almost universal popularity somewhat mysterious.

occur all the time in nature.[41] And when these horrors are not haunting our sentient cousins in the wild, the fear and struggle to avoid them are. There is rarely a moment of peace in the perpetual struggle for survival that life in nature is. And, as if this were not enough, there is also r-selection, the reproductive strategy of most non-human animals, where beings have huge numbers of offspring — sometimes even millions of individuals for every set of parents — and only few of these survive to reproduce themselves. (Given that the population remains stable, there will on average only be two out of the thousands or millions of individuals who will survive long enough to reproduce themselves.) The rest will either be eaten, die from starvation, or have their life ended in another horrible way before they can manage to create an equally waste- and painful circumstance as the one they were brought into themselves. So, most regrettably, the reality of life in nature is that most non-human animals are merely born to suffer and die.[42]

These realities of life in the wild provide us convincing reasons to believe that suffering is overwhelmingly predominant for sentient life in nature.[43] In other words: that nature is an unacknowledged hell. This

---

[41] These horrors of course also haunt many humans, but fortunately we have realized that they are worth preventing in the case of humans, and for that reason we have also managed to reduce them. The next step is to do the same in the case of non-human animals.

[42] Suffer, because what else can describe a life lived in fierce competition all about getting food and avoiding getting eaten between thousands, or even millions, of siblings, only two of which survive on average?
And those who do survive to reproduce will of course suffer a similar fate too, often only shortly after their siblings have all died. Many fish, for instance, die shortly after they have spawned.

[43] To be sure, I am not claiming that joy and pleasure is not found in nature too. It surely is, as Jonathan Balcombe shows in his book *Pleasurable Kingdom*. Yet the sad truth remains: suffering is overwhelmingly predominant in nature.

conclusion may not be easy to accept, and for those who are not yet convinced, I recommend consulting the material found in the following note.[44] But once we acknowledge this conclusion, we are bound to accept its obvious implication: we must do something to reduce suffering in nature. We *should* intervene in nature.[45]

Again, in the case of humans who suffer from ills such as starvation and disease, we realize that we have an obligation to help, and to refuse to expand this realization to non-human beings amounts to nothing but speciesism. Nonetheless, even people who seek to

---

[44] A presentation by Oscar Horta: https://www.youtube.com/watch?v=cZ0XTofuGmY
Articles by Horta: http://www.animalcharityevaluators.org/blog/why-the-situation-of-animals-in-the-wild-should-concern-us/;
https://masalladelaespecie.files.wordpress.com/2012/05/debunkingidyllicview horta.pdf;
https://masalladelaespecie.files.wordpress.com/2011/09/disvaluenatureinterve ntion.pdf; http://digitalcommons.calpoly.edu/cgi/viewcontent.cgi?article=1114&context=bts
Presentation by Adriano Mannino & Ruairí Donnelly:
https://www.youtube.com/watch?v=4aa6g1y4l8I
The seminal paper by Yew-Kwang Ng that coined the term 'welfare biology' and seeded that still grossly underdeveloped field:
http://www.ntu.edu.sg/home/ykng/Ng1995 welfare bio.pdf
Essay by Brian Tomasik: http://foundational-research.org/publications/importance-of-wild-animal-suffering/
Essay by Catia Faria: http://blog.practicalethics.ox.ac.uk/2014/12/should-we-intervene-in-nature-to-help-animals/
Essay from veganism.com: http://www.veganism.com/should-humans-help-free-living-animals/

[45] This conclusion of course does not *depend* on nature being full of suffering, since we should do what we can to minimize suffering regardless — even just relatively small amounts of suffering would still be worth preventing via intervention, given that such intervention minimizes net harm. What the fact that the amount of suffering in nature is overwhelming makes clear, however, is that suffering in nature is an enormous problem that demands urgent priority, and that intervention is an imperative of the highest order.

transcend speciesism will often still refuse to accept this conclusion,[46] and will try desperately to avoid it with all sorts of objections, and I shall therefore respond to the most common of these objections below, and try to show why they fail.[47]

"But suffering in nature is natural. It's all part of the circle of life, and we should not disturb that."

That something may be considered part of "nature" or "natural" does not imply that it is good or normative, not even remotely. After all, evils such as disease, starvation, and violence can all be considered natural and part of nature,[48] yet we are not tempted to defend them on those grounds, at least not when they haunt humans, in which case we realize that we should give up romantic and ethically misguided notions about not "disturbing nature", and instead act on the basis of that which is truly valuable: preventing harm and suffering. And,

---

[46] Similar to the way in which "conscientious" omnivores sedate themselves with the fairy tale of happy non-human animals on farms, most so-called (non-human) animal advocates seem equally guilty of indulging in an, if possible, even more naïve and sedative fantasy, namely the fantasy of the happy non-human animals in nature.

[47] The following objections are all modified versions of actual objections that have been put forth in favor of letting nature be. Ironically, most of them come from vegans who claim to care deeply about non-human animals. I beg them to think harder about what genuine care actually demands.

[48] *"But only humans are violent. Other animals are only 'violent' toward beings they eat."*
False. Lions and chimpanzees often kill their own kind, sometimes they proceed to eat them, sometimes not; many cats, including house cats, often kill other animals only to leave their carcass to rot; seals have been observed raping penguins; and one could keep on mentioning examples. "Happy, peaceful nature" is a myth, and it is time we stop entertaining it. It does non-human animals no good to ignore the cruelties of nature and the harm they impose upon each other and themselves, quite the contrary.

again, to not extend this insight to non-human animals is simply speciesist. Refusing to relieve hunger or cure a disease that is tormenting another person, whether human or non-human, is indefensible, and insisting on this refusal with reference to the fact that these ills are part of "nature" or "the circle of life", does not make it less so. The wish to preserve Mother Nature as she is merely reflects a failure to realize what a horrible mother she is: the kind that eats herself mercilessly.

If we view things from the perspective of the non-human individuals in nature, it becomes even clearer just how apathetic this romantic "don't disturb the circle of life" attitude actually is. Consider this: If you were the victim who were about to be disemboweled and eaten while still alive, would you then have any gratitude for being part of "the circle of life"? Would you then have any objections against other people "disturbing nature" in order to save you from such torment? Of course not. You would most certainly prefer not to be in that situation in the first place, and to be helped in case you were, and it is nothing short of delusional to believe that the sentient non-human beings who become such victims every day have a different preference.

"Non-human animals in the wild can sustain their populations without our help, so there is no need for us to interfere."

This again reflects the speciesist attitude of conservationism, namely that population sustainment is what is normative for non-human beings, a view we are not tempted to entertain in the case of populations of humans. Moreover, the fact that a group of beings can sustain their numbers at relatively stable level does not suggest that their lives are not full of suffering — indeed, as any appreciation of r-selection makes clear, such sustainment rather suggests the opposite — and nor does it imply that we should not intervene in order to help them. For instance, human societies struck by disease, starvation, and war can usually also "sustain their population" at a relatively stable level, yet we should nonetheless clearly "intervene" and relieve their harm and suffering when we can. Again, what matters is the well-being of sentient individuals, not that populations of certain kinds of individuals are sustained.

"Predators cannot be held morally responsible, and they need to kill in order to survive. Besides, nature isn't cruel, it just is. Cruelty is a human-made concept."

A brick that falls down on someone's head with skull crushing effect is not cruel either, but it has bad consequences nonetheless, and the harm it causes is certainly worth preventing, whether we deem it cruel or not. The same is true of the harm found in nature. As for the other point this objection raises, the problem of predation, it is first worth noting that this problem is only part of the broader problem that is suffering in nature, and that any discussion that makes suffering in nature exclusively about the problem of predation clearly betrays a lack of serious thinking about this extensive problem. After all, even if predation could be removed by the snap of a finger, starvation and disease would still be endemic in nature. The amount of suffering in nature would still be of incomprehensible magnitude.

As for predators' need to kill in order to survive and their lack of moral responsibility, let us remove all biases in favor of certain species of predators and the wonder of nature by leveling the playing field entirely — with humans. Imagine we have a group of humans who are unable to perform any moral reasoning (as some humans are), and who can only survive by killing and eating other humans; say, about one human every week. Now, with all speciesist and nature revering biases out of the way, we can ask the question: should we really do nothing about this situation? Should we just let these humans go on to kill a human of their choice every week? Or should we rather prevent these humans from killing other humans, and instead provide them with a sufficient substitute for the human flesh they need to survive? As is hopefully clear to anyone, the latter is by far the better option. What changes, then, when we substitute the beings in this thought experiment with beings of another species, essentially getting us back to the problem of predation in nature? Nothing, unless we entertain speciesism.

"As humans, we only have an obligation to prevent the suffering that humans cause. The rest is not our responsibility."

This is a speciesist position. Again, we realize that we have an obligation to help save humans from disease, starvation, and predation, and the fact that these ills are not caused by humans is irrelevant. The same is true when they strike non-human individuals. Moreover, the notion that we only have an obligation to prevent suffering caused by humans is wholly arbitrary, and only repeats the mistake of putting special emphasis on the human species compared to the rest of the animal kingdom. Because, after all, I could equally say that, as a Danish citizen, I only have an obligation to prevent the suffering caused by Danish citizens, the rest is not my responsibility. That would be just as senseless and arbitrary. Why draw such arbitrary distinctions? Why pretend that suffering caused by disease, natural disasters, or predators is less worthy of prevention than suffering caused by humans? There is no good reason. It is merely an excuse to escape the enormous responsibility we have to help prevent sentient beings from suffering. *That*, and nothing less than that, is our true responsibility.[49]

"Who are we to say whether non-human animals in nature need or want our help?"

Who are we *not* to say this? Who are we to be so cold and apathetic as to look at someone who is starving or eaten alive, and then say that we don't know whether they would have preferred avoiding the suffering they are experiencing? Just as we can say that non-human animals are better off spared from our confining, mutilating, and killing them, we can also say that they are better off not starving and not disemboweled. Those two judgments require exactly the same minimum amount of common sense.

"Humans should not dictate how other animals live. It is imperialistic, an expression of imagined human supremacy, and way beyond what we have the right to do."

---

[49] The subtext of this objection seems to be that only "deliberately caused" suffering should be prevented. As just stated, this view is false, but more than that, it is also worth noting that the moment we can do something about suffering in nature, as we already can now to some extent, the suffering we fail to prevent is in fact due to human deliberation. The suffering we fail to prevent happens due to our *deliberate* omission to reduce the suffering we could and should prevent, no less than the drowning of a child whom a group of bystanders chooses not to save is due to human deliberation. In fact, we are exactly such bystanders with regard to non-human animals who suffer in nature. We see them suffer, yet we just stay put and let the cameras role.

Is it imperialistic to save a human from the teeth and claws of a predator? Or is it only so when the victim is a non-human individual? Is it imperialistic and "beyond what we have the right to do" to cure non-human animals from diseases that plague and kill them? Consider rinderpest, for example, a disease that used to plague and kill many kinds of ungulates, including antelopes, giraffes, warthogs, and wildebeests, but which we have now cured. How dare we dictate these beings to live free of this horrible disease? What gave us that right? No, the question is rather: How can we justify not taking such actions that can relieve the suffering of beings in nature when we have the power to do so? And on what grounds could anyone defend opposing such benevolent interventions?

The objection that we do not have the right to interfere is as misguided as can be, because on no conceivable notion of rights could one reasonably claim that we do not have the right to prevent other individuals from being harmed. The whole point of rights is to protect beings and their interests from being harmed, which is exactly what the interventions in question are all about. And not only do we have the right to relieve others' suffering; we have a duty to do so.

"Talking about helping non-human animals in nature while we abuse and kill billions of them ourselves is just absurd. We should end our abuse of them first, and then we can start talking about the issue of suffering in nature."

While this objection may seem wise at first sight, it is actually anything but. It is deeply speciesist, and to see how this is so, it is again worth directing our focus to humans, the beings whom we tend to think the most clearly about in moral terms, and whom our moral intuitions do not allow us to disregard merely because they find themselves categorized as "being in nature".

So let us again replace non-human individuals with humans in the morally problematic scenario before us so as to rid ourselves of any speciesist bias that we may be blind to. We then get the following scenario: billions of humans are enslaved, exploited, and killed by a certain group of humans (the one we belong to) every year, while an untold number of trillions — thousands of billions — of humans live in nature where they suffer and die in horrible ways. They suffer from disease, parasitism, starvation, and from killing and eating each other. Now, say we are a minority of people within the oppressive group of humans, a minority that is against enslaving and exploiting others, and that opposes suffering in general. Is it really obvious that we should focus almost uniquely on the billions of humans exploited and enslaved by our own group, and not dedicate much focus to the other humans who suffer — the vast majority, more than 99 percent of them — as long as our own group is exploiting humans? No, it is not obvious. In fact, what is obvious is that such an attitude is completely indefensible. We cannot defend ignoring suffering merely because it is not caused by humans, and this conclusion applies equally to the suffering of non-human individuals in nature. The fact that humanity is exploiting billions of sentient beings gives us absolutely no reason to ignore the suffering of trillions of such beings in nature.

It does of course make good sense to grant disproportionate attention to the beings whom we are exploiting, both because ending this exploitation and the suffering it causes is relatively straightforward — all it requires is that we decide to end it — and because our collective ethical attitudes with regard to non-human animals cannot be anything but misguided as long as we exploit and consume non-human animals. That being said, we should still be careful not to fall prey to the illusion that 50 billion beings who are the victims of human exploitation matter more than 50 billion beings in nature, an illusion that does seem disturbingly widespread.

It should be pointed out that, far from being innocent, the sentiment expressed in the objection above could easily end up having extremely harmful effects. For example, we might well be able to alleviate suffering for innumerable beings in nature before we can end all enslavement and exploitation of non-human individuals by humans, which could well take centuries if we are talking about *all* exploitation.[50] In fact, as the case of alleviating rinderpest shows, this is clearly possible: we obviously can reduce suffering for non-human animals in nature, even when most people collectively support the exploitation and killing of non-human beings. Should we postpone similar efforts of researching into how we might relieve suffering for non-human individuals — perhaps for trillions of them — until we have ended all humanity's enslavement and exploitation of such beings? This seems an untenable position, yet that is what the objection above suggests.

The objection above also seems to rest on the fallacious assumption that there is a conflict between taking seriously the suffering of non-human beings in nature and then taking seriously the

---

[50] And if this notion of *all* exploitation is a straw man, where exactly lies the boundary below which our abuse of non-human animals is small enough for us to focus on non-human individuals in nature? Note that my point is not that the goal of ending all human abuse of non-human individuals is not an immensely worthy one — it sure is — but simply that we have to take the suffering of *all* beings seriously and address the suffering of all beings with urgency, not only that of beings whom humans are exploiting.

suffering of the beings whom we are exploiting, which in practice means ending our exploitation of them. This is misguided, because if anything, it is actually helpful, required even, that we take the suffering of non-human animals in nature seriously in order to bring an end to our own abuse of non-human animals. Because as long as we maintain that the suffering of non-human animals in nature does not merit serious consideration and intervention, we will inevitably embrace and reinforce a starkly speciesist position, a position that does not grant sufficient moral consideration and respect to the interests of non-human animals and the plight of their suffering. And, needless to say, such an attitude is exactly the very foundation of our exploitation of non-human animals.

Thus, far from being in conflict with the goal of ending our exploitation of non-human animals, granting adequate moral consideration to non-human individuals in nature, and being clear about the implications of doing so, actually seems paramount for this end. A failure to grant such consideration will only perpetuate our moral confusion and speciesism.[51]

In conclusion, it makes sense to give disproportional focus to the beings whom we are exploiting, yet it is not the case that we need to wait for the end of all human exploitation of non-human beings in order to investigate and employ ways to help non-human beings in nature. Both non-human beings who live in nature and non-human

---

[51] It is of course true that the relationship goes the other way too: we will not take non-human individuals in nature seriously enough as long as we exploit them ourselves, and therefore the suffering of non-human individuals in nature only underscores the importance of veganism. Consequently, what we need to do is simply to cut to the root: to reject all speciesism and act on the implications of doing so. To both end our exploitation of non-human individuals *and* take seriously the suffering of non-human individuals in nature.

beings who are exploited by humans matter, and we cannot defend only taking the suffering of one of these two groups seriously.

"We should not intervene in nature, because we would only mess things up and cause more harm than good."

First note that this is not an objection against interventions in nature that reduce suffering, but rather an objection that holds such interventions to be impossible in the first place — a contention that is clearly untrue. Because as the earlier mentioned example of our eradication of rinderpest shows, we clearly can take actions that reduce harm for non-human animals, and these need not "mess things up" in any way. And one can point to countless other examples of indisputably good interventions: a guy who swims out to save a duck who is about to drown in a frozen lake,[52] a group of people that saves two elephants — a mother and her baby — from dying in a mud pool,[53] a group of friends who save a moose from freezing to death in ice cold water,[54] etc.

According to the objection above, none of these interventions should ever have occurred, which clearly reveals its speciesist stance, since we would never suggest that it is acceptable to leave humans to drown, freeze to death, or in any other way suffer and die when we can help them, and claiming that it is acceptable, even normative, not to do anything when such calamities befall non-human individuals is nothing but speciesism in vigorous action.

---

[52] See http://www.boredpanda.com/duck-rescue-frozen-lake-norway/

[53] See http://www.dailymail.co.uk/news/article-2059502/Baby-elephant-mother-pulled-muddy-grave-conservation-workers-Zambia.html

[54] See http://www.veganism.com/category/helping-animals/page/3/

Yet the problem with the objection above is not only speciesism, but also defeatism, an indefensible surrender and faith in powerlessness in the face of the mountain of suffering found in nature (and this nasty mountain is something that this objection against messing things up clearly does not appreciate, since the truth is that nature is already "messed up" and full of harm). However, this defeatism of course has its roots in speciesism too. For never are we tempted to respond in such a presumptuous and defeatist manner in the face of human suffering. When it comes to human suffering and its causes, we do not make lazy and apathetic claims à la: "we should not intervene, because we will only cause more harm than good", or "there are too many unforeseen consequences, so it is best just to leave it alone". This would not be our reply if it were trillions of humans who were eating each other alive and otherwise suffering and dying in horrible ways.

No, in the case of human ills, we rightly realize our obligation to take action. Smallpox, for instance, killed hundreds of millions of people in just the 20th century alone, and we rightly realized it was bad. We then successfully eradicated it, and we saw it was good. No sane person can look at the picture of someone suffering from smallpox and claim that its eradication was not a good thing, and no sane person would have argued against curing it out of a fear of unforeseen consequences. This is not how we respond to the plight of human suffering. Why, then, would we respond differently to the plight of the suffering of non-human animals in nature?

As the example of smallpox perfectly shows, paralyzing ourselves from alleviating suffering with fears of unforeseen consequences cannot be defended. No doubt it makes good sense to worry about unforeseen consequences, and to think about what consequences our actions might have in the worst case, yet we cannot allow the prospect of unforeseen consequences to paralyze us, give up, and leave the suffering of others alone. After all, we can never know what the exact consequences of our actions will be, and thus our actions are in fact guaranteed to have unforeseen consequences, regardless of what we do, which means that the insistence not to act in the face of a risk of unforeseen consequences simply amounts to an insistence not to act at all. This is not a viable option in the real world, especially not when we are faced by an emergency. And this is indeed what suffering in nature is: the greatest emergency on Earth.

The only excuse there is for not supporting ambitious human intervention against suffering in nature is not knowing how bad the state of nature is for non-human animals, which is actually no excuse at all. The amount of suffering that occurs in nature every second is beyond comprehension, and a rejection of speciesism requires that we stop entertaining lazy rationalizations in defense of ignoring and leaving this suffering alone, and that we instead start taking it seriously. Upon rejecting speciesism, there is no way we can defend not doing anything about the suffering of non-human animals in nature, the vast majority of suffering taking place on Earth. We must do what we can to spare non-human individuals from harm.

INTERVENE HOW?

So, given that we must do what we can to reduce suffering in nature, the burning question then becomes: *How can we best help reduce the suffering of non-human animals in nature?*

That is indeed the question, an open and difficult question for sure. Fortunately, the first step toward answering this question, and actually also the first part of the answer to the question itself, is quite obvious: *we must acknowledge the importance of the question and try hard to answer it.* An obvious point, perhaps, but by no means an insignificant one. For instance, just consider what the implications would be if humanity accepted this answer and worked hard on finding out how we can best reduce the suffering of non-human animals. Getting to this point might well be the single most important step we could take toward the goal of reducing the suffering of non-human animals, since all other good steps we can take likely will follow and be made much smoother by that foundational step.

Unfortunately, this seems the only answer to the question that we can state with certainty. Aside from getting humanity dedicated toward this goal, it really is an open question what we can do to improve the condition of sentient life in nature as much as possible. There are of course the obvious actions such as curing diseases and saving individuals trapped in freezing lakes or mud pools. But although such interventions are surely good, and something we should do if possible, they are not significant in the bigger picture. Even if we could successfully cure the worst disease that plagues non-human animals right now, suffering would still be endemic in nature and largely undiminished in the aggregate. Little would be changed. The problem of suffering in nature is a big one, and we must remember that the question is not merely whether we can do *something* to improve the state of things. Rather, the question is: what is the *best*, most *effective* thing we can do? How can we reduce the most suffering and make the greatest positive impact for sentient life in nature?

Broadly speaking, there seems to be two different kinds of answers one can give to this question, both of which should be viewed as hypotheses about how we might be able to improve the condition for sentient life in nature as much and as effectively as possible. The first option is to *alter* sentient life on the planet, while the second is to *phase it out*.

These appear the only options there are. If we find it unacceptable that non-human animals eat each other and that they give birth to thousands of younglings only for that same number of thousands minus a few to die in pain shortly after birth, as we indeed must if we reject speciesism,[55] then we have no choice: we must either drastically *change* sentient life and the way it presently unfolds on our planet, or *phase it out*.

Philosopher David Pearce has outlined and argued for an approach of the former kind: the abolitionist project, as he calls it, which is an ambitious project that aims to redesign all sentient life on Earth by

---

[55] Again, we would never accept if these things happened to humans.

means of genetic engineering and nanotechnology in order to abolish suffering and magnify well-being throughout the living world.[56] Such a project may sound far-fetched, yet one should keep in mind the reality that motivates such an exotically sounding project before one surrenders to aversive intuitions against it, that reality being the horrible suffering that takes place in nature as it is right now, and which will continue to take place if we leave it alone. Pearce provides a simple thought experiment that may help expose our biases against the project: Imagine that we encountered an alien civilization that already had carried out the abolitionist project and thus phased out suffering in their ecosystems, leaving only flourishing beings on their planet. Would we then, when meeting these aliens, insist that they should undo what they had done and urge them to reintroduce suffering — reintroduce parasitism, predation, r-selection etc.? It seems that we would be quite misguided in such an insistence, which suggests that an insistence against carrying out a similar project on our own planet, where suffering is presently the default, merely arises from status quo bias: the bias toward favoring things as they are because that is how they are rather than because of a good reason.

One may of course be skeptical about the feasibility of the abolitionist project, yet it is important to distinguish such skepticism from opposition to the project on principle, i.e. opposing it even if it is feasible. It surely is an open question whether the abolitionist project

---

[56] Writings by Pearce on the abolitionist project and the redesigning of sentient life:
http://abolitionist.com/
http://www.hedweb.com/abolitionist-project/reprogramming-predators.html
A video with Pearce talking about redesigning nature (contains disturbing images):
https://www.youtube.com/watch?v=KDZ3MtC5Et8

will be both technically and sociologically feasible, but according to Pearce himself, the greatest challenges the project faces are not found in the technical realm, but rather in the sociological — in convincing humanity to pursue this project. And *if* suffering ends up being optional, a technical problem we can solve if we so choose, it would indeed be beyond indefensible not to make the choice to abolish it and replace it with something better.

The alternative to altering sentient life is to phase it out, a suggestion that may sound even more controversial and even more radical than redesigning it. One proponent of this approach is philosopher David Benatar who in his book *Better Never to Have Been* argues that coming into existence is always a harm, and thus that bringing someone into this world can never be justified, at least not for the sake of that someone; a position known as anti-natalism. In presenting his argument, Benatar focuses mainly on humans, yet the argument applies to all sentient beings who have the capacity to suffer — which would include all sentient beings presently living on Earth.[57] Many reject Benatar's anti-natalist conclusion out of hand because it clashes with some of the most fundamental values and attitudes we hold. Yet

---

[57] Note, however, that the argument would not apply to sentient life that had successfully undergone the abolitionist project that David Pearce advocates. In fact, Benatar's main argument, the so-called asymmetry argument, gives the opposite conclusion in the case of such flourishing beings who are unable to suffer and who are brought into a world without suffering, since one both avoids harm by bringing such a being into the world, which is good, a plus in Benatar's asymmetry matrix, and one brings joy into the world, which is also good, another plus on Benatar's matrix. That ends up being ++, which is better than the single plus that Benatar assigns to not bringing sentient life to the world (Benatar's simple matrix: https://shaunmiller.files.wordpress.com/2011/06/positive-and-negative-values.png).

while this may be true when speaking of humans, the same cannot be said in the case of the majority of non-human animals in nature, where the case for the anti-natalist position is much stronger. In fact, one could even argue that in the case of most beings in nature, the anti-natalist conclusion follows directly from a rejection of speciesism: by simply applying the most basic ethical sense that we would apply to human reproduction.

For instance, only one out of eight lion cubs survive into adulthood, while the rest die in horrible ways, e.g. due to disease, starvation, or, not uncommonly, being killed by a male lion who wants to have some fresh cubs of his own with the mother of the cubs he is killing. Is that a prospect we would ever accept in the case of humans? Would we allow ourselves or any other human to go ahead and reproduce if we *knew* the odds to be that, on average, seven out of eight children would be sure to die a horrible death within the first couple of years? It seems safe to say that we would not, or at least that we should not. And yet lions by no means constitute an extreme or even representative example of how likely non-human individuals are to reach adulthood in nature. For a more representative example, consider the prospects of newly hatched salmons.[58] A salmon can lay more than 5,000 eggs, the majority of which will hatch as small younglings called alevins, and out of these thousands of young fish, less than 50 will survive the first year, while only two will survive

---

[58] This is a more representative example because the biggest group of vertebrates in terms of the number of individuals is fish, which outnumbers mammals by at least 10 times, and likely more than 100 (again, see http://reducing-suffering.org/how-many-wild-animals-are-there/). If one considers invertebrates too, the average number of offspring that dies shortly after birth becomes even greater still, since invertebrates tend to have a much higher number of offspring.

long enough to reproduce themselves. Again, we can ask whether we would ever allow any human to reproduce given such a statistic, and this time the answer should be even clearer than before. Surely, we would never allow anyone to give birth to a thousand human children if we knew that only about ten of them would survive the first year, so how can we defend taking another stance when it comes to non-human children?[59]

It may again be helpful to challenge any status quo bias that could be hiding in the corners. Imagine there were no salmons on Earth. No salmons struggling, starving, or getting eaten alive. No cycle of life, pain, and death for these sentient individuals. Would we, in light of such an absence of salmons, feel any obligation to bring such beings and their struggle and deprivation into the world if we could? Hardly. If anything, it seems we would have an obligation to not bring such harm into existence, which suggests that our current acceptance of things as they are — the presence of salmons and our wish to preserve them — is not a well-reasoned position, but a preference for things as they are because that is the way they are. Status quo bias.

"But would preventing non-human animals from procreating not amount to an infringement of their right to procreate? And would it

---

[59] What about Benatar's argument that coming into existence is *always* a harm, implying that procreation, even under the best of circumstances we can find today, cannot be justified? This is a complex question, and it lies beyond the scope of this book to answer it. The relevant argument here is that even if we take the bare minimum of common moral sense we have with regard to human procreation and apply it to non-human procreation — essentially that we apply a non-speciesist ethic of procreation — the conclusion is that we should prevent (at least) most non-human animals in nature from procreating if we can (for a more elaborate statement of this argument, see *The Speciesism of Leaving Nature Alone, and the Theoretical Case for "Wildlife Anti-Natalism"*).

not effectively amount to global human oppression of the rest of the animal kingdom?"

Can anyone meaningfully claim a right to procreate if their act of procreation is guaranteed to lead to massive harm for others? If one does defend a right to procreate, it seems that one must acknowledge that it has certain limits just as any other right. Presumably, we should at least maintain that "the right to procreate is limited, as other rights are limited, by the threat of harm to others."[60] And for the vast majority of non-human animals in nature, serious harm and early death to others — the "others" being the majority of individuals who will be brought into existence by the act of procreation — is not merely highly likely, but a *guaranteed* consequence of procreation. And given such a guarantee, it does not seem justifiable to maintain a right to procreate. Human or non-human, the act of bringing new beings into existence when it is a certainty that the overwhelming majority of these beings will suffer short, brutish lives cannot be defended.

As for the claim about human oppression, the point of preventing non-human animals from procreating would not be to oppress or harm other beings, but rather the opposite: to spare them the torment they would suffer by being brought into the world in the first place. And it should go without saying that preventing procreation is not the same as, nor even comparable to, killing a being, which surely is a harm,[61]

---

[60] Quoted from: http://plato.stanford.edu/entries/parenthood/

[61] *"But is killing necessarily a harm? What if it is done painlessly?"*

As any study of methods that are meant to kill painlessly makes clear (see for instance Derek Humphry's *Final Exit*), there is no sure way to bring about a painless death in the real world, and that fact alone puts this notion that killing is not a harm to sleep for good. Sentient beings do not come with any off button. They come with resilient bodies, all of them different, and all of them programmed to take up a tough fight for life almost regardless of what is thrown at them, be it cyanide, bullets, or high voltage. For more elaboration on oppressive, and, to put it simply, *wrong*. Preventing beings who will live short lives of deprivation from coming into existence is the exact opposite of that: it is to prevent harm and death, including the process of dying. The whole point of preventing the creation of non-human animals who are doomed to live short, horrible lives is to spare *them*, not us. After all, what serves humans the most is arguably the laissez-faire approach to nature, since that means devoting as little focus and resources as possible to the betterment of the lives of non-human individuals in nature, and reserving it all for humans. Yet such self-serving conduct requires a certain kind of stilts in order to stay balanced: speciesist ones.

Just as it is not oppressive or ableist to prevent certain physically impaired individuals from driving a car when they cannot do it safely, and hence are likely to harm others by doing it, it is not oppressive or speciesist to prevent non-human beings from procreating when such procreation is guaranteed to result in massive suffering and early death for others, those others being their own younglings. As argued above, what would be speciesist would rather be to allow such grotesquely harm creating actions if we can prevent them.[62]

---

the harm of death, see https://www.utilitarianism.com/magnus-vinding/harm-death.html.

[62] *"But what about the ecosystem? Doesn't it need all these beings?"*

As mentioned earlier, the view that we should preserve non-human individuals — essentially that we should be willing to sacrifice them — for the sake of keeping the ecosystem stable is an instrumentalist view of other sentient individuals that is deeply speciesist, one we would never entertain in the case of human individuals. What ultimately matters is sentient beings and their well-being, and ecosystems only matter to the extent they are instrumental to *that*. Hence, it is not that keeping the ecosystem stable is necessarily irrelevant, but that it is relevant to the extent it is valuable for sentient beings — the kinds of beings this objection appears ready to sacrifice for the sake of the ecosystem, when it should be the other way around.

That is of course the thing: *if* we can. Presently we cannot safely prevent non-human animals from bringing new beings into an unworthy existence of suffering and early, brutal death. For while there are humane methods that can prevent at least many kinds of non-human animals from reproducing, such as sterilization and so-called sterile insect technique,[63] it makes little sense to employ these to only a few species, since that would likely just lead to a compensating rise in populations of other species, thereby leaving the net change of such interventions close to zero, possibly even negative.

No matter what we may choose to do in order to reduce suffering in nature, any significant reduction of suffering will require carefully planned, large-scale actions, kinds of actions that seem to lie well beyond what we can readily do today.

In conclusion, it remains an open question what we should do about the suffering in nature, and the preliminary and obvious answer likely remains both the only certain and most important one at this point: we should work on finding out how we can best reduce suffering in nature. No matter which of the two kinds of approaches — the redesigning or the phasing out/fertility regulating approach — or any combination of the two, the task is the same: we must examine the problem before us in depth and seek possible solutions and ways to implement these. Again: *we should work on finding out how we can best reduce suffering in nature.*[64]

---

[63] See http://en.wikipedia.org/wiki/Sterile_insect_technique

[64] For more on how to work for a future with fewer harms to non-human beings in nature, see: http://www.animal-ethics.org/working-for-a-future-with-fewer-harms-to-wild-animals/.

A SHORT NOTE ON INSECTS

As stated earlier, moral consideration, and hence also *insufficient* moral consideration, including discrimination, pertains only to *sentient* beings, which renders the question concerning which beings are sentient a crucial one. As I have noted earlier and argued elsewhere,[65] it seems safe to assert that all vertebrates and at least some invertebrates, such as cephalopods, are sentient, but beyond that, the matter is less clear. What about invertebrates with relatively small brains such as insects?

The honest answer is that we don't know. The only way we can solve the problem of other minds, at least functionally, and at least for now, is by analogy to other beings: by observing them at the behavioral and neurophysiological level and comparing this to our own neurophysiology and behavior that we know is accompanied by sentience. And in the case of insects and other arthropods, such analogies are generally difficult to draw. However, our failure to draw such analogies does not imply that these beings are not sentient. Indeed, we cannot exclude that they might be *intensely* so.

So the short answer is that we do not know, yet there is much to

---

[65] See the first part of *A Copernican Revolution in Ethics*.

add to this short answer. First, as noted earlier, we have little reason to believe that the number of neurons found in the brain is of the greatest relevance when it comes to the presence and intensity of experiences. As noted earlier, more than half of the neurons in the human brain are found in the cerebellum, a brain structure that does not seem to play a big role for our conscious experience, if any at all, while a minority is found in the cerebrum, whose activity most aspects of our conscious experience, if not all, seem to depend upon.

What this basically tells us is that more neurons in a live brain does not necessarily imply "more sentience", and that it is brain *function*, not size, that is the most relevant factor when it comes to sentience. Based on this observation, we seem to have good reason to be open-minded about the possibility that sentient experiences, intense ones even, are present in relatively small brains like those of insects.

On the other hand, the case of the seemingly unconscious cerebellum can also support an argument in favor of the opposite proposition, namely that insects are not sentient at all. Because what it appears to prove is that the complex workings of enormous clusters of neurons that assists in the coordination and execution of bodily movement, which appears to be the primary function of the cerebellum, need not result in sentience, which implies that some complex mechanical coordination, perhaps including that of insects, might well take place entirely "in the dark". These are worthwhile, yet wholly inconclusive speculations.

In contrast, one particularly bad argument against insect sentience that no one should fall for is that they do not possess the specific neurophysiological structures that give rise to sentience in humans and other vertebrates, and hence they are not sentient. This is a non sequitur, because, unlike what this deduction assumes, it is no law of nature that only vertebrate nervous systems can give rise to sentience. Indeed, there is absolutely no reason to suppose that other kinds of nervous systems cannot give rise to sentience as well, especially given the fact that convergent evolution is relatively common.[66]

Another problematic argument against insect sentience worth criticizing is that there is no evolutionary reason for sentience to evolve in insects. Because insects tend to live short lives, live in large groups, and generally have a very limited capacity for learning, and because sentience is found at the individual level and serves a function in learning, insects are not sentient. This is indeed a thin argument.

First, the fact that many insects live in big groups where individuals will tend to sacrifice themselves for the sake of the group does not mean that individual insects do not feel pain. For the most part, even in the case of the most social insects, individual insects need to navigate in the world in a way that preserves their own existence, and in that situation pain could well evolve and make sense in evolutionary terms. Just as the fact that some human individuals have sacrificed themselves for their own tribe does not imply that these individuals could not feel pain, we cannot infer that insects feel no pain because they tend to willingly sacrifice themselves for the sake of the group.

Second, the claim that insects are not sentient because their capacity to learn is not advanced seems specious to say the least, first of all because many insects, including bees and cockroaches, indeed

---

[66] Of course, if they had sufficiently similar structures and functions to those that underlie sentience in ourselves, we could be sure that they are sentient, yet the fact that they do not does not allow us to make a deduction in the opposite direction, and assert that they are not sentient. That simply does not follow. There might be more than one way to Rome.

do display quite advanced learning abilities, and second, because it is not at all clear that any advanced learning ability is necessary in order for sentience to arise. In the case of humans, for instance, who are certainly both sentient and learning beings, the function of, say, intense pain does not seem to only, or even mainly, relate to learning. For example, do people with severe amnesia who are unable to learn new information lose the ability to feel anything? Are they unable to feel intense pain? The answer is "no". Rather, the function of intense pain is motivation, a motivational signal that inherently carries the message: **do something now!** There does not seem to be any requirement for an advanced ability to learn in order for such a message to exist and be effective in a being, nor does there seem to be any reason why such a signal could not have evolved in insects.

Since insects and other small beings are so alien to us, it is only to be expected that we have a hard time thinking clearly about them, and that our thinking on the matter of insect sentience and ethics is fraught with bias. This obviously poses a problem for our attempt to be reasonable about this important subject, yet we can, however, create tools that help us think better, and in the case of biases and other fundamental missteps in our thinking, the golden tool is to become aware of these pitfalls in the first place. There are of course many biases that influence our thinking about insects and other small beings, not to mention our thinking in general, but it seems to me that the following three biases/missteps are especially worth pointing out and being aware of in order for us to think clearly about this complex and important matter, and to avoid jumping to conclusions prematurely:

1. Sizeism

We appear to have a tendency to consider smaller beings "less sentient" and less morally important than bigger ones. It somehow *feels* like a lobster is much more likely to be sentient than, say, an ant. However, this intuition is far from justified, since an ant brain actually has more than twice as many neurons than the brain of a lobster, while bees and cockroaches both have about ten times as many neurons as a lobster. So, when we think about insects and small beings in general, it is worth planting this flag in the front of our minds: we should not be swayed to believe that these beings matter less simply because they are small.

2. Our Convenience

The bias against small beings seems closely related to another bias we have, namely the bias to believe what is most convenient. For it would no doubt be much more convenient if small beings such as insects are not sentient. If they are, and if they can feel pain, the world suddenly becomes very complex and messy, and not least full of suffering beyond what we have imagined thus far. Therefore, it seems reasonable to suspect that our reasoning is somewhat motivated to jump to the conclusion that insects are not sentient, which then gives us all peace of mind and stops arousing our present view of the world. Yet we cannot allow ourselves to estimate what is true based on what feels the most comfortable to us, and therefore we should be acutely aware of this tendency.

3. In Comparison to Us

Lastly, there is the tendency to believe that insects do not matter because their brains are so much smaller and contain far less neurons than human brains do. As we shall see below, if one looks at the total neuron count, insects actually vastly outnumber humans in the neuron number game, yet the problem with the belief in question is much deeper than this. For whether a being matters is not contingent on what other beings they share the world with and how complex these other beings are. To see that this is true, consider what would happen if we suddenly encountered aliens with brains much larger than human brains, highly sentient brains containing trillions of neurons. Would humans suddenly not matter upon encountering such beings? Would the intrinsic value of human life suddenly be diminished? Of course not. Humans matter just the same and are just as valuable no matter what kinds of other beings that exist in the world, and this holds true of all sentient beings. The moral value of sentient beings is *intrinsic* in their sentience, not contingent.[67] Big-brained beings do not render beings with smaller brains less valuable than they are.

The bottom line is that we must take seriously the possibility of sentience in insects and other small beings, and take seriously the potentially enormous obligation and moral importance found in this realm. Because given how numerous insects are — it is estimated that there are around 10^{18} to 10^{19} on the planet — they could well constitute the majority of intrinsic moral value on the planet. In fact, unless insects are not sentient at all, they seem to constitute such a majority

---

[67] For a short defense of the absoluteness of moral value, see the essay 'The Felicific Continuum: Absolute or Not?' in my book *Moral Truths: The Foundation of Ethics*.

almost no matter what standard one chooses to evaluate by. Take the absolute number of neurons, for instance, which is often held against them — their low number of neurons compared to other beings. If we assume an average neuron count of 10^5 in insects, then this gives us that, based on the lower estimate above, there are a total of 10^{23} insect neurons on the planet. Compare that to the number of neurons found in humans: there is just short of 10^{10} humans with just short of 10^{11} neurons each, which gives us that there are less than 10^{21} human neurons on the planet. Thus, according to these estimates, there are more than a hundred times more insect neurons on the planet than there are human neurons. One can of course dismiss such an absolute count as being a poor indicator of moral value, but then what is a better such indicator? Should brain-to-body mass ratio be factored in too? If so, this only favors insects even more, since they generally have large such ratios, much larger than humans. Small ants, for instance, have a brain-to-body mass ratio of 1:7, while it lies around 1:40 in humans.

Not even the suggestion that insect sentience is highly uncertain does much to change the conclusion. Because even if we hold that the probability that insects are sentient in a way comparable to humans is extremely low — say, 0,0001 percent — then, in utilitarian terms, the expected value found in the insect realm will still be enormous, and even for very low such probabilities, this value will still vastly outweigh that which is found in humans. In the case of the specific estimate 0,0001 percent, the expected value, as obtained by multiplying our probability with the number of insects, will still be at least a hundred times greater than the value found in the human realm today.[68] No matter how we look at it, insects appear likely to matter. A lot.

How we should act in light of this conclusion is largely an open question. Yet given that insects usually have enormous numbers of younglings, the vast majority of which die after a short while, there seems to be strong reasons to believe that the vast majority of insects are better off never being born, and that we therefore ideally should prevent their births — a conclusion echoed by Brian Tomasik, perhaps the foremost thinker on the subject of insect suffering: "I would dread being born as an insect, and I would wish that others would prevent my birth".[69]

---

[68] Could one not apply the same reasoning to plants? One could, but the conclusion would be different, because, unlike what desperate rationalizers of the exploitation of non-human beings maintain, the probability that plants are sentient is ridiculously, Planck scale low. Insects have a nervous system that moves their body around, plants have nothing, and do nothing, remotely like it. The difference is total.

[69] Quoted from http://reducing-suffering.org/speculations-on-population-dynamics-of-bug-suffering/
See also: http://reducing-suffering.org/do-bugs-feel-pain/

TRANSCENDING SPECIESIST LANGUAGE

In order to transcend speciesism, we must transcend speciesist language. This is an important task, since the way we speak strongly influences the way we think and act. For example, by referring to a non-human individual with pronouns such as "it" or "something", we erroneously categorize this being as an insentient object, and such language cannot be reconciled with a sufficient degree of moral respect for sentient beings, and cannot avoid having harmful effects.

By analogy, consider how harmful it would be if we began referring to certain races of humans as "its" or "somethings". It is plain to see that this would be deeply racist, an instance of overt discrimination, and yet it is in fact no less discriminatory and respectless when we use such words when referring to non-human individuals; we just fail to see it because such language is so commonplace. This is how we normalize and trivialize speciesism: we repeatedly talk about non-human animals as though they were insentient objects, thereby continually pulling them in the direction of the "insentient object" category in our minds. And when a group of beings has this unfortunate status, we will not be moved to have proper concern for them. This is why we must stop referring to non-human individuals as "it" or "something", and instead use the pronouns that express recognition of the fact that they are sentient individuals — a *s/he* and a *someone*.

Our speciesist language is not limited to pronouns, however, which is just the tip of the iceberg. There is also the harmful practice of name-calling, which often, if not most of the time, employs the names of certain non-human animals in a pejorative way. *Pig, cow, chicken, sheep, weasel,* or simply *animal*. The examples are countless, and the role they play is the same in each case: the denigration of, and clear expression of disrespect for, non-human individuals. To call someone a "pig" or "weasel" reflects a low view of such non-human beings, and serves to further perpetuate and reinforce such a low, speciesist view. It is really no better and no less discriminatory than to call someone a "paki" or "nigger".[70] And just as one cannot challenge racism while using such racist language, one cannot challenge speciesism while using speciesist language.

There are also the countless euphemisms that we employ, and which help disguise the personhood and value of non-human beings, and consequently these euphemisms blind us to the horror and death we bring upon non-human individuals. For example, the flesh of non-human beings has nothing but euphemistic names. People eat "beef" rather than the flesh of a cow, "pork" rather than the flesh of a pig,

---

[70] After all, the word "nigger" comes from the Latin word for black, and used to be a neutral word, and it is exactly because of its derogatory use that it is now a racist word, and the same is true of "paki", which derives from Pakistani: it is only racist because it has been used in a disparaging way. One may wonder whether we will one day refer to pigs, cows, chickens, and sheep with other names and view these old ones as forever smeared by their use in speciesist ways. One can only hope.

"chicken" and "fish" rather than the flesh of *a* chicken or *a* fish. This way of referring to body parts of non-human individuals as though their flesh is all that they are is a typical example of speciesist language — speaking as if there is no being there, just a thing. Unfortunately, such speciesist language is even found in vegan food shops, where one can order vegan foods with names such as "tuna sandwiches" and "chicken burgers". Calling foods such names does not exactly serve to question speciesism and the view that non-human beings are mere food. Rather, it reinforces it.

Important to note, however, is that we not only employ speciesist euphemisms and distracting language to disguise human exploitation of non-human beings, we also use these to disguise the horrors of nature. For example, we say that predators "prey upon" their "prey", which is a rather euphemistic way of putting the process of someone getting ripped and bitten to death. Moreover, calling someone "prey" also completely fails to reflect respect and compassion for the individual who is being killed and eaten, and it is surely not a word we would use when referring to a human who suffers such a horrible fate of being chased down and killed.

Another way in which we perpetuate speciesism with our words is with our use of common expressions that signify non-human beings to be inferior to human beings, and which suggest exploitation and abuse of non-human individuals to be legitimate. As Joan Dunayer writes:

> Some human-nonhuman comparisons convey disrespect *only* toward other species. *Work like a horse* expresses concern, even admiration, for a human worker but

suggests that horses rightly toil for humans. *Human guinea pigs* voices sympathy for humans unwittingly used as experimental subjects, and indignation over their unjust treatment, but implies guinea pigs are appropriate victims.[71]

Or perhaps the most telling example of all: *I was treated like an animal.* This expression implies that horrendous treatment of non-human beings is "normal" — not something that we would ever question. Moreover, it suggests that humans and animals are two fundamentally different groups, as opposed to the former being a subset of the latter, and thus it serves to otherize and "dehumanize" — or rather "deindividualize"[72] — non-human animals. As Carl Sagan and Ann Druyan rightly noted: "A sharp distinction between humans and 'animals' is essential if we are to bend them to our will, make them work for us, wear them, eat them — without any disquieting tinges of guilt or regret."[73] Indeed.

We need to break this distinction down, and therefore we should avoid referring to non-human individuals simply as "animals", which preserves this gap, and rather use terms such as "non-human animals", "beings", or "other animals". After all, calling certain races of humans for "animals" is also taxonomically correct, yet applying such language only to some races is clearly racist and "otherizing".

---

[71] Dunayer, 2001, p. 166.

[72] That is after all what we mean by the word "dehumanize" — to rob someone of their status as a sentient, feeling individual.

[73] Sagan & Druyan, 1993, p. 365.

One could keep on mentioning examples of speciesist language,[74] yet the few ones mentioned above hopefully make the point clearly enough: speciesism is ubiquitous in common language, and it is important that we become aware of this, and that we also start challenging speciesism on this level so that we can stop perpetuating it with our words.

---

[74] For a book-length treatment of speciesist language, see Joan Dunayer's *Animal Equality: Language and Liberation*.

IS ANTI-SPECIESISM ANTI-HUMAN?

Let us finally address this worry: Does ending speciesism imply that we should care less about humans? The answer is simple: No way. To say that it does would be like saying that ending sexism means caring less about individuals of a certain gender, the gender one used to consider morally privileged, or that ending racism implies less moral consideration for any race otherwise considered morally privileged. It is a total non sequitur. Ending discrimination does not amount to lowering anyone in moral terms, but rather to raising everyone. Raising everyone to proper moral status.

In a nutshell, ending speciesism simply means that we give proper moral consideration to non-human beings. It implies that we grant them greater moral consideration than we presently do; not that we should grant less moral consideration to humans. After all, our moral concern for other humans is clearly not where it should be either. Millions of children die of readily preventable diseases every year, and yet most of us seem to devote more attention to the latest movie release than to such human tragedy and the question of how it can be relieved. So, clearly, we need to grow ethically *on all fronts*. And growth on one front need not happen at the expense of growth on another. It is possible to raise the moral tides so that concern for all beings is heightened. That is what true moral progress is, and what we should pursue going forward.

EPILOGUE: WE ARE ALL SPECIESISTS

No group of humans has ever been held in as low regard or exploited on anything close to the same level as non-human beings have been throughout history and still are today. No group of humans has ever been systematically bred, raised, killed, and eaten. No group of humans has ever been born and raised in order for people to make basketballs, wallets, or boots out of their skin. No, there is no comparison. No group of humans has ever truly been "treated like animals".[75]

This says something about how deep the problem of speciesism is and how big the challenge of overcoming it is. In terms of overcoming discrimination, it is an unprecedented challenge in the history of humanity. And the reasons this challenge is so big are both obvious and vitally important to see.

---

[75] And notice how the worst atrocities committed against humans are often described in this way: "We were treated like [non-human] animals." (For example, I recently heard a Holocaust survivor utter these very words.) Yet when people draw comparisons in the other direction, comparing the way we treat non-human beings to the worst of atrocities committed against humans, this is often seen as unfair and sensationalist. So how come it is accepted to draw this comparison one way, from human to non-human, but not the other? What explains this asymmetry? Speciesism. Because we have realized that enslaving, numbering, and killing human individuals is pure evil, and we have yet to realize that this is just as true in the case of non-human individuals.

The first reason is that we are humans, and as humans we are disposed to feel moral concern primarily for other humans. Consequently, for most of us, it will likely be much more difficult to get our moral sentiments kindled by the suffering of non-human beings than by that of humans. That is what one would suspect based on our evolutionary history, and the reality about how humans in all cultures view and treat non-human beings bears this suspicion out.

The second reason is the culture that we as speciesist beings have constructed and which we keep on reinforcing. We talk about non-human beings as though they are things, and as though they have no considerable value, and we exploit and abuse them as commodities. We literally consume them and products of their suffering on a daily basis. One could hardly devise a more powerful propaganda against concern for non-human beings than these insidious everyday practices.

So this is why the challenge is so massive: we have a strong disposition not to be as concerned for non-human beings as we are for human beings, and, largely due to this disposition, we have created an extremely speciesist culture that serves to foster the ugly potential of this disposition. And the reason it is important to realize this is that it reveals the remedy for going beyond speciesism, namely *a cultural shift*. This is obvious, because of these two factors — our dispositions and our culture — the only one we can change today is our culture. By creating a better culture, we can inhibit our unfortunate dispositions and reduce the harm they cause. We have done this before, and we can do it again. Indeed, a cultural shift away from speciesism appears to be taking place already, albeit slowly, and there is no reason to believe that this shift cannot keep on advancing further. After all, the ethical inclusion of all of humanity that seems widespread today was itself adopted quite recently, and if we can expand our ethical inclusion this much, so much that we rightfully include a child on the other side of the planet in our sphere of moral concern, at least in the abstract, then why should we not be able to do the same thing with a bird or a fish on the other side of the planet? When looked at from that perspective, this extra step no longer seems that radical or undoable.

In order to bring about this cultural shift away from speciesism, it seems to me that we must be honest and admit the reality of our condition: that we are all speciesists. On many levels even.

First, at the level of our innate moral psychology, we should admit that we all have the above-mentioned disposition. Our mind tends to react stronger to the plight of human suffering than it does to the plight of non-human suffering, and the latter will likely often fail to even trigger much of a reaction at all in many people. For instance, most people seem able to watch a lion kill and eat a zebra without being deeply moved, while images of a human who suffers the same fate generally will provoke much stronger reactions.

Running away from this fact about ourselves and pretending we have no such disposition does not help non-human beings. On the contrary, ignoring it only makes us confused about the problem we are facing and what its roots are. Rather, what we need to do is the exact opposite: to acknowledge this disposition and plant the knowledge of our biased moral intuitions in the front of our awareness. That is the first step toward overcoming such a bias. And not only does such knowledge make the problem we are facing clearer, it also reveals what the solution is at the level of our minds. Because given that our moral intuitions are biased against non-human beings, it becomes clear that we cannot trust these intuitions — our moral sentiments, or *gut feelings* — to take us beyond speciesism. Instead, we must turn to our friend *reasoning*.

Our moral sentiments will tend to scream that humans exist in another, much higher realm of moral value than non-human beings (and, although it is rarely stated explicitly, this also seems the greatest source of resistance against arguments in favor of granting full moral consideration to non-human beings: it just *feels* wrong). Yet by following reasoned arguments over unreasoned intuitions (which, to be sure, I fully share), we see that such screams are unfounded. Their basis lies in our evolutionary history and cultural consensus, not in reason. Hence, the most important precept to follow in our effort to get beyond speciesism could well be this: avoid being too fast to trust your (screaming) gut feeling. And by following this precept and careful reasoning about the matter, especially by continually asking how we would feel and act if *x* were human(s), we might eventually be able to cultivate moral intuitions that do reflect moral wisdom with regard to non-human individuals too, along with a social intolerance toward speciesism that is as great as our intolerance toward discrimination against humans. That would seem to be the way to counter our unfortunate speciesist disposition and the speciesism it fosters. Indeed, nothing less than this will do: we must cultivate better moral intuitions and social norms altogether, since overcoming speciesism is not just a matter of rejecting a certain propositional belief, but a matter of rejecting and overcoming a pervasive *attitude* deeply rooted in our mind and society.

Second, on top of our biased intuitions, we are also all speciesists because we have been raised in a speciesist world full of speciesist words, entertainment, education, etc. Speciesism is everywhere in our everyday lives, in every aspect of our culture. For this reason too, it seems naive to believe that one can completely avoid being speciesist in all aspects of one's words and conduct, or completely distance oneself from all speciesist ideas and practices any time soon. After all, it is still an open question what aspects of our culture and practice that are speciesist, and what the practical implications of rejecting speciesism are in the first place, and even many people who have thought much about speciesism seem to get these implications profoundly wrong.

None of this gives us reason to give up and surrender to speciesism, of course. On the contrary, it underscores the importance of keeping on being on the outlook for speciesist tendencies in our culture and in ourselves, and to keep on investigating the implications of rejecting speciesism so that we can work our way toward the end of it — a project that has only just begun. This book has been an attempt to further and spread this project.

WHAT CAN YOU DO NOW?

Plenty. If one is new to veganism, an introduction can be found at vegankit.com. Beyond that, one can read more about speciesism and related subjects on pages such as animal-ethics.org, sentience-politics.org, and end-of-speciesism.org, and in the resources I have linked to throughout this book and in the bibliography. One can spread awareness of the issue by educating others about speciesism, and about why it is wrong and what follows from its rejection. One can connect with other people who are interested in the subject of speciesism and ethics, like people in the so-called Effective Altruism community, and discuss the implications of rejecting speciesism with them. Given that speciesism is so pervasive, and given that the movement against it is so young, even a relatively small effort can make a big difference at this point.

ACKNOWLEDGMENTS

This book has been inspired by writings and/or presentations by the following six stars of benevolence: David Pearce, Brian Tomasik, Oscar Horta, Yew-Kwang Ng, Adriano Mannino, and Ruairí Donnelly. I owe them all my thanks. I'm especially grateful to Oscar who, apart from delivering the talk that prompted me to write this book in the first place (this one: https://www.youtube.com/watch?v=v_vsHlKZPFQ), provided helpful suggestions and comments.

Special thanks must also go to David for his ever cheerful encouragement that, like his unbelievable compassion and intellect, never ceases to inspire me. How can one help but feel deep admiration and affection for such a beautiful soul? I certainly can't.

Lastly, I'm grateful to my friends Joe and Jess for many inspiring discussions about these issues, for making me think deeper, and for making the period in which I wrote this book a pleasant one in wonderful company. Jess also suggested edits that improved the quality of the book. Thank you both very much!

BIBLIOGRAPHY

Balcombe, J. (2006/2007). *Pleasurable Kingdom: Animals and the Nature of Feeling Good.* Basingstoke: Macmillan.

Bastian, B., Loughnan, S., Haslam, N., Radke, H.R.M. (2012). Don't Mind Meat? The Denial of Mind to Animals Used for Human Consumption. *Pers Soc Psychol Bull.* 38(2), pp. 247-256.

Bekoff, M. (2007). *Animals Matter: A Biologist Explains Why We Should Treat Animals with Compassion and Respect.* Boston New York: Shambhala Distributed in the United States by Random House.

Benatar, D. (2006). *Better Never to Have Been: The Harm of Coming into Existence.* Oxford New York: Clarendon Press Oxford University Press.

Berridge, K.C. & Kringelbach, M.L. (2011). Building a neuroscience of pleasure and well-being. *Psychol Well Being.* 1(1): pp. 1-3.

Churchland, P. (2011). *Braintrust: What Neuroscience Tells Us about Morality.* Princeton, N.J: Princeton University Press.

Darwin, C. (1872). *The Expression of Emotion in Man and Animals.* Oxford, England: Appleton

Davidow, B. (2013). Why Most People Don't Care About Wild-Animal Suffering. reducingsuffering.org. Retrieved from: http://reducing-suffering.org/why-most-people-dont-care-about-wild-animal-suffering/

Dawkins, R. (2011, June) 'Richard Dawkins on vivisection: "But can they suffer?"'. *boingboing.net.* Retrieved from: http://boingboing.net/2011/06/30/richard-dawkins-on-v.html

Donaldson, S. & Kymlicka, W. (2011). *Zoopolis: A Political Theory of Animal Rights*. Oxford England New York: Oxford University Press.

Dunayer, J. (2001). *Animal Equality: Language and Liberation*. Derwood, Md: Ryce Pub.

Francione, G.L. (1999/2011). *Introduction to Animal Rights: Your Child or the Dog?* Temple University Press.

Greek, J. & Greek, C. (2004). *What Will We Do If We Don't Experiment On Animals? Medical Research for the Twenty-first Century*. Victoria, B.C: Trafford.

Griffin, D.R., Speck, G.B. (2004). New evidence of animal consciousness. *Anim Cogn*. 7(1), pp. 5-18.

Horta, O. (2010). What Is Speciesism?. *Journal of Agricultural and Environmental Ethics*. 23, pp. 243-66. Retrieved from: https://masalladelaespecie.files.wordpress.com/2010/05/whatisspeciesism.pdf

Horta, O. (2010). Debunking the Idyllic View of Natural Processes: Population Dynamics and Suffering in the Wild. *Télos*. 17, pp. 73-88. Retrieved from: https://masalladelaespecie.files.wordpress.com/2012/05/debunkingidyllicviewhorta.pdf

Horta, O. [EffectiveAltruismCH] (2013, May). Oscar Horta: Why animal suffering is overwhelmingly prevalent in nature. Retrieved from: https://www.youtube.com/watch?v=cZ0XTofuGmY

Horta, O. [Jean Pierre Froud] (2013, September). Oscar Horta - About Strategies. Retrieved from: https://www.youtube.com/watch?v=v_vsHlKZPFQ

Inmendham [graytaich0]. (2011-2015). 'Best Work'. Youtube playlist by graytaich0. Retrieved from: https://www.youtube.com/watch?v=b1mJnEmjlLE&list=PLcmZ9oxph4sxzDfr2oH6tpNij-YUH5dy3

Inmendham [CrownJules84]. (2013, February). Gladiator War (Graphic Content). Retrieved from: https://www.youtube.com/watch?v=bK2a-1K0Sdg&t=8s

Knight, A. (2011). *The Costs and Benefits of Animal Experiments*. Palgrave Macmillan.

Low, P., Panksepp, J., Reiss, D., Edelman, D., Swinderen, B.V., & Koch, C. (2012). 'The Cambridge Declaration on Consciousness'. Retrieved from: https://web.archive.org/web/20131109230457/http://fcmconference.org/img/CambridgeDeclarationOnConsciousness.pdf

Mannino, A. & Donnelly, R. [frei denken uni basel]. (2014, January). Reducing Wild Animal Suffering. Retrieved from: https://www.youtube.com/watch?v=4aa6g1y4l8I

Masserman, J. H., Wechkin, S., & Terris, W. (1964). "Altruistic" behavior in rhesus monkeys. *Am J Psychiatry.* 121, pp. 584-585.

Ng, Y-K. (1995). Towards Welfare Biology: Evolutionary Economics of Animal Consciousness and Suffering. *Biology and Philosophy.* 10, pp. 255-85. Retrieved from:
http://www.stafforini.com/library/ng-1995.pdf

Pearce, D. (1995/2007). *The Hedonistic Imperative.* Published online at: http://www.hedweb.com/hedab.htm. PDF download:
https://cl.nfshost.com/david-pearce-the-hedonistic-imperative.pdf

Pearce, D. (2009). 'Reprogramming Predators'. *hedweb.com.* Retrieved from: http://www.hedweb.com/abolitionist-project/reprogramming-predators.html.

Pearce, D. (2012). 'The Anti-Speciesist Revolution'. *hedweb.com.* Retrieved from:
http://www.hedweb.com/transhumanism/antispeciesist.html

Pearce, D. (2016). Compassionate Biology: How CRISPR-based "gene drives" could cheaply, rapidly and sustainably reduce suffering throughout the living world. Retrieved from: https://www.gene-drives.com/

Raup, D. (1992). *Extinction: Bad Genes or Bad Luck?* New York: W.W. Norton.

Regan, T. (1983/2004). *The Case for Animal Rights.* Berkeley: University of California Press.

Regan T. (2005). Criminalizing Vivisection. *tomregan.info.* Retrieved from http://tomregan.info/criminalizing-vivisection/

Ryder, R. (1972). "Experiments on Animals", in Stanley and Roslind Godlovitch and John Harris. *Animals, Men and Morals.* Grove Press, Inc.

Sagan, C. & Druyan, A. (1993). *Shadows of Forgotten Ancestors: A Search for Who We Are.* New York: Ballantine Books.

Slovic, P. (2007). "If I look at the mass I will never act": Psychic numbing and genocide. *Judgment and Decision Making.* 2(2), pp. 79-95.

Speciesism: The Movie. (2013). Film. Directed by Mark Devries. Mark Devries Productions.

Tomasik, B. (2009a/2014). 'The Importance of Wild-Animal Suffering'. *utilitarian-essays.com*. Retrieved from: http://www.utilitarian-essays.com/suffering-nature.html

Tomasik, B. (2009b/2014). 'The Predominance of Wild-Animal Suffering over Happiness: An Open Problem'. Retrieved from: http://reducing-suffering.org/wp-content/uploads/2014/10/wild-animals.pdf

Tomasik, B. (2009c/2014). 'How Many Wild Animals Are There?'. *reducing-suffering.org*. Retrieved from: http://reducing-suffering.org/how-many-wild-animals-are-there/

Tomasik, B. (2012/2014). 'Suffering in Animals vs. Humans'. *utilitarian-essays.com*. Retrieved from: http://www.utilitarian-essays.com/suffering-in-animals-vs-humans.html

Tomasik, B. (2013a/2014). 'Speculations on Population Dynamics of Bug Suffering'. *utilitarian-essays.com*. Retrieved from: http://www.utilitarian-essays.com/bug-populations.html

Tomasik, B. (2013b/2014). 'Applied Welfare Biology and Why Wild-Animal Advocates Should Focus on Not Spreading Nature'. *utilitarian-essays.com*. Retrieved from: http://www.utilitarian-essays.com/applied-welfare-biology.html

Vinding, M. (2014a). *Why We Should Go Vegan*.

Vinding, M. (2014b). *Why "Happy Meat" Is Always Wrong*.

Vinding, M. (2014c). *A Copernican Revolution in Ethics*.

Vinding, M. (2014d). *Moral Truths: The Foundation of Ethics*.

Vinding, M. (2015). 'The Harm of Death'. Retrieved from: https://www.utilitarianism.com/magnus-vinding/harm-death.html

Vinding, M. (2016a). *The Speciesism of Leaving Nature Alone, and the Theoretical Case for "Wildlife Anti-Natalism"*.

Vinding, M. (2016b). 'Animal advocates should focus on antispeciesism, not veganism'. Sentience Politics. Retrieved from: https://sentience-politics.org/animal-advocates-focus-antispeciesism-not-veganism/

Vinding, M. (2017). *You Are Them*.

Printed in Great Britain
by Amazon